A forager's guide to

Wild Drinks

A forager's guide to

Wild Drinks

Ferments, infusions
and thirst-quenchers
for every season

Liz Knight

Illustrated by
Veronica Ballart Lilja

Contents

Summer

Making the drinks

Rewilding your drinks

Do you have a selection of herbal teas in your kitchen? You know the types: little boxes of tea bags filled with apparently magical combinations of herbs, spices, fruits, roots and maybe even mushrooms. One might claim to help you sleep and another to calm nerves or to boost your immune system. Or perhaps you have shelves filled with things more alcoholic – bitter fortified wines and flavoured spirits to turn into cocktails, or liqueurs made from delicious fruits, flowers or herbs.

The chances are that if you do, there will be more than a few wild plants in those little tea bags or bottles – linden to calm, hops to aid sleep, burdock to cleanse, wormwood to add bitterness to vermouth or juniper to make gin.

Just as your tea cupboard and your less puritanical drinks shelf are filled with wild plants, so many other drinks have long been laced with the flavours and benefits of wild ingredients. And although those in the know might prefer there to be an air of mystery about the plants they blend, you'll often find the herbs that make it into those drinks are actually rather common, and – more often than not – growing nearer to you than the shops you bought them from.

This book has been written to introduce you to these plants. Whether your drink of choice is tea, coffee, non-alcoholic (or alcoholic) ferments, infusions, liqueurs or juice, this book will guide you through a year of harvesting and turning your plants into delicious beverages. You will slowly replace the shop-bought boxes and bottles with home-harvested products.

Along with information about where, when and how to harvest your finds, the book includes two recipes for each plant. Treat them as a base to experiment with and remember that the flavour of wild ingredients is not uniform. Your soil, weather and altitude will make your plants taste different to mine. Have confidence in your tastebuds; if something is too sweet, add sourness and, above all, have fun experimenting!

Before you start

There are a few important things you need to remember before you start, in order to create safe and sustainable drinks. Firstly, and perhaps most importantly, *never* consume anything you are not 100 per cent convinced you have correctly identified. Start with the plants you know and slowly build up your knowledge of

the other plants around you. Remember plants often have different names across the world and different plants can share the same common names, so it's worth cross-referencing your finds with their scientific names to make sure you're looking for the right plant. Be aware that the illustrations in this book are not botanical identification guides. Invest in a pocket book of plants in your local area to help correctly identify your plants (see page 266 for some recommendations).

When you first introduce a new plant into your diet, use small amounts at first. Just as you can react to conventional ingredients, people can with wild plants too. They often have therapeutic, medicinal properties that are beneficial to most, but if you have a medical condition, or you are on certain medications, some plants may exacerbate your condition or counteract the effects of your medicine. While this book includes some of the cautions, you should investigate which plants are safe for you to consume. This advice also applies to pregnant women.

Get to know the legal restrictions on harvesting in your area or country; cities and regions may have their own foraging rules. Avoid harvesting where there might be contamination in the ground from industry, spraying or other activities – graveyards, for example, are potentially full of heavy metals and are best avoided for wild food.

You might be legally allowed to harvest a plant, but ask yourself before you do whether it is ethical. Only harvest from areas where there is an abundance of non-endangered plants, and only gather what you need. A good forager gathers lightly, aware that every plant plays an important role in the ecology of an area.

While most plants will be in easy reach, using a jar of juniper berries or a bunch of thyme from a shop is absolutely fine. If you are lucky enough to have your own garden or even a small back yard, you can fill it with many of the plants in the book.

Now dust off your demijohns, clear space in your cupboard for jars of herbs, find a spot on your work surface for ferments to bubble and a corner of your drinks cabinet for homemade liqueurs to steep, and watch as your drinks turn wildly delicious.

Spring

Spring often seems to arrive almost overnight with its sudden plume of warm, sweet air enticing people out of their homes. With its blossoms and lush carpets of new growth, there's no other season that has such a definitive arrival and neither is there one so anticipated. Offering a feast of ingredients for wild drinks, spring is the time to brew fresh herbs in teas, to smash leaves into rejuvenating cocktails, to blend them into detoxifying juices and to capture its very essence in liqueurs, wines and vinegars.

Birch
Betula spp.

With their iconic white bark, birch may be easiest to identify in the winter, but it's on the cusp of spring that the tree is most revered. One of the first trees to come into leaf, birch is associated in many cultures with the arrival of spring. For foragers, it is the tree that starts the new gathering year because for a few weeks each spring birch trees are tapped for their sap, which starts to circulate around the tree as the days warm up, providing nutrients, water and sugar to kickstart it into life for the new year.

It's not just the sap of the tree that is edible or useful though; birch bark, twigs, leaves and catkins are all full of unique flavours and benefits – including flavonoids, saponins and tannins – all of which are at their highest concentration at the very start of spring. The perfect start for a year of drinking in the wild.

Edible parts: Bark, leaves, twigs, catkins and sap. Birch also hosts medicinal fungi including chaga and polypore.

Harvesting: Gather birch buds through the winter; only take bark from fallen trees or branches. The sap starts rising as the days warm: break a twig from the end of a branch and droplets of sap will appear at the break. You can harvest it by drilling into the tree, but a less intrusive way is to cut the end of a branch and push a bottle over the cut end, tying it onto the tree. When the leaves start opening, the sap stops dripping and becomes bitter. The leaves and catkins can be harvested in spring and summer.

Pairs with: Nettle, rosemary, ground ivy, mint, pine, dill, chervil, flowering currant, primrose, rhubarb, vodka, schnapps and gin.

Locations: Woodland and grassland in temperate and cooler climates. Birch sap is most successfully harvested in areas with a hard frost.

Caution: Make sure to use clean tools if you drill into the sap wood and only drill into mature trees.

How to drink: birch

Birch sap is full of minerals and vitamins and, when freshly harvested, it tastes faintly sweet. It ferments very quickly into a sour, yeasty, cloudy liquid – storing it in the freezer will keep it fresh to drink when the sap has stopped rising.

Wine: Birch sap wine is light, dry and refreshing. Although the sap will start to ferment by itself, using a wine yeast will ensure that it has a good flavour.

Liqueurs: Birch bark, sap and leaves can all be used in liqueurs. Drinks producers distil the sap into a spirit or dilute the sap 50:50 with a high proof (100%) neutral spirit (this is how you can do it at home). Some are made by soaking the leaves or twigs in a spirit or by blending sap syrup with it.

Cordials/syrups: Birch sap needs to reduce down to around one-eightieth of its original volume to become a syrup, a very small yield. Add an unrefined sugar or sweetener to speed up the process and increase the volume. If your sap has started to ferment, reducing it with a sweetener works well.

Tea: Infuse birch twigs into a decoction-style tea. Leaves can be used through the spring and summer – younger leaves are most fragrant and green tasting, while older leaves are more tannic.

Fermented drinks: Birch sap will often start to ferment after 24 hours of being harvested. It quickly becomes sour before it can develop any fizz so use it in conjunction with other sweet ingredients. The sap is a perfect base to make fermented drinks such as kombucha. In Slavic countries, it is preserved by making it into a kvass-style drink. The bark is also used in lightly fermented drinks, including Canadian birch beer. Similar to root beer, this is made from birch sap flavoured with bark extract along with vanilla and cinnamon.

Bitters/tinctures: A combination of birch twigs and young leaves makes delicious bitters. Pack a jar with twigs and freshly opened leaves and cover with a neutral spirit. If you infuse them for a few days, you will have astringent, tannic and fresh-flavoured bitters. But leave them to soak for a few months before straining, and the woody, sweet flavours will be released, making it so smooth you could almost drink it neat.

Promise of spring

Once you sip freshly harvested birch sap, you'll know it's a very special drink. While you can turn it into all manner of drinks, sap deserves to be celebrated as it is, lightly laced with a few other delicious flavours that hail the beginning of spring and the new foraging year.

──────

SERVES 4
1 litre (1³/₄ pints) fresh birch sap
4 birch twigs, about 10cm (4in) long,
    rubbed to expose the inner green layer
15g (¹/₂oz) nettle leaves
15g (¹/₂oz) cleaver stems
Sweet violet flowers and leaves, and/or
    primrose flowers, to decorate

Pour 100ml (3¹/₂fl oz) of the sap into an ice cube tray and freeze. Pour the remaining sap into a jug and add the twigs, leaves and stems and leave to soak for 2 hours.

Divide the violets and/or primrose into four flat-based glasses with the birch sap ice. Strain the sap into the glasses, then push one of the twigs into each glass to decorate. Raise your glass to toast the coming year of wild drinks.

Spirit of birch

Most of us probably only have a single birch tree to collect sap from, and only a few hours to do it. Fortunately, you can turn what might seem to be a tiny harvest into something quite special. Freezing the sap not only allows you to make the drink sweeter, but also keeps it fresh until the leaves start opening.

──────

MAKES 700ML (1¹/₄ PINTS)
1.5 litres (2³/₄ pints) fresh birch sap
6 birch twigs, about 10cm (4in) long,
    leaves starting to open
400ml (14fl oz) high-proof vodka
10 rosemary leaves, the tip of a stem (optional)
10 sweet violet flowers (optional)
1 tablespoon sugar syrup or xylitol (optional)

Place the sap in a plastic box with a lid and place in the freezer. Put the birch twigs in a wide-necked jar and pour over the vodka. Add the rosemary and violets, if using, and leave to macerate for 2 hours. Strain the infused vodka into a sterilized bottle.

Remove the sap from the freezer and thaw until 300ml (¹/₂ pint) of the sap has become liquid. This part will have more sweetness than the remaining ice as sugars thaw at a lower temperature. Pour the thawed sap into the bottle with the flavoured vodka.

The liqueur will be faintly sweet – if you wish to sweeten it, add sugar syrup, if you have any, or the xylitol sweetener (which is made from the sugars in birch trees). This drink will store indefinitely but is best drunk within a few weeks of opening.

Sweet violet
Viola odorata

These tiny violet flowers would be easy to miss if it weren't for the fact that they all seem to appear at the same time. The flowers grow on slender stems from the centre of little heart-shaped leaves. All violets are edible but some are more perfumed and delicious. These are sweet violets (*Viola odorata*) and, although all violets are perfectly useful in teas, only the sweet violets will create perfumed drinks.

The odourless wild violets have hairless stalks, whereas perfumed sweet violets have tiny, downy hairs growing along them. Once you've found your sweet-smelling violet, you might discover that the flower suddenly loses its perfume and you are plunged into doubt about your find. Don't panic – wait a few minutes and smell the flower again. If you can smell the sweet scent once more, you have definitely got the right flower. The scent comes from a chemical called ionone which, as well as smelling sweetly, can shut smell receptors off before stimulating them again, tricking your brain into thinking that the smell is new each time.

Edible parts: Leaves, stems and flowers.

Harvesting: The taste of violets is so alluring that in many places, wild violets have become scarce. Fortunately, violets are easy to grow in gardens, even in pots, so create your own perfumed garden by planting violets under trees and watching them creep across your lawn, turning it into a sweetshop of flowers in the spring.

Pairs with: Nettle, cleavers, rosemary, tree syrups, vanilla, mango, almond, orange, gin, cherry, lemon, chocolate, tea, rose, mint, blueberry, blackberry, milk and vermouth.

Locations: Dappled woodland, alkaline, calcium-rich grasslands and garden lawns.

Caution: African violet (*Saintpaulia ionantha*) is not the same species as sweet violet and is not known to be edible.

How to drink: sweet violet

These flowers are sweetly floral with an almost rose-like flavour. The leaves are fresh, nutty and slightly peppery. If you want only the sweetness of violets, just use the petals, removing any green parts from them.

Wine: The ancient Greeks and Romans used violets for pain relief and as a hangover cure, ironically infusing them into honey-sweetened white wine.

Beer: Some craft beermakers add violet flowers or Parma violet flavours to their brews. To see why, add a drizzle of violet syrup to your pint. It tastes especially good in light, citral beers.

Liqueurs: Violet flower liqueurs can be made by simply infusing the flowers (removing any bitter green parts) in vodka or brandy. Sweeten with sugar, light honey or a light maple syrup.

Cordials/syrups: Violet syrup is a wonderful way to capture the sweet essence of violet. Sweet violet liqueurs and syrups are stalwarts of a well-stocked cocktail bar; use in everything from the classic Aviation, to Martinis, Gin Sours and Champagne cocktails.

Tea: Fresh and dried violet flowers and leaves are delicious in either cold or hot tea. To get the maximum flavour and benefits from hot tea, use slightly cooled boiled water, leaving the flowers and leaves to steep for a few minutes. Violets are lovely blended with nettles and cleavers in tea or added with rose petals to black tea.

Warming/milky drinks: These are made heavenly with the addition of violets. Add a spoonful of syrup or violet sugar, stir and enjoy your soothing mug.

Fermented drinks: Violet flowers are beautiful added to the second fermentation of kombucha, kefir and jun. Add the flowers to lightly fermented nettle beer for a springtime flavour.

Salts/sugars: Violet sugar has a long shelf life and can be used to decorate the rims of cocktail glasses or as a sweetener. Simply blend fresh violet flowers with sugar, dehydrate (see page 234) and blend again to a fine powder.

Sweet violet syrup

Syrups have been used since the medieval period for flavouring food, drinks and medicines. Violet syrup was the first ever pH indicator (experiment yourself by turning the syrup blue with alkaline soda water, or pink with acidic lemon). Try stirring a spoonful into ice-cold milk or making an alcohol-free sour cocktail by shaking together 1 tablespoon of syrup with 2 tablespoons of lemon juice, 50ml (2fl oz) of apple juice, an egg white and some ice.

MAKES 200ML (7FL OZ)
25g (1oz) violet flowers (about 2 handfuls)
150ml (5fl oz) water
150g (5oz) white sugar

Wash the flowers and pinch them from the tops of the stems, making sure you remove any green parts of the plant as these are bitter and would affect the flavour. Place the flowers in a container. Boil the water and leave to cool for a few minutes before pouring 75ml (2½fl oz) over the violets. Cover, and leave to steep overnight.

The next day, place the sugar and remaining water in a saucepan and slowly heat, stirring, until the sugar has dissolved. Bring to the boil, heating until the syrup is clear. Take the syrup off the heat and allow to cool for 5 minutes before stirring in the violet and water infusion. Leave for a couple of hours before gently warming the syrup and straining through a fine sieve. (The strained flowers can be dried and used in baking or drinks.) Pour the syrup into a freshly sterilized bottle. This syrup will keep for up to 3 weeks in the fridge.

Violet crème liqueur

Most modern violet liqueurs use artificial flavours, but the original violet drinks such as Crème Yvette and Parfait d'Amour are flavoured with more natural ingredients: spices, fruits and other flowers, and this is a little nod to these drinks of old. This recipe calls for blackberries, which aren't in season at the same time as violets, but you can use frozen blackberries or frozen or dried violets, depending on if you're making the drink in spring or autumn.

MAKES 700ML (1¼ PINTS)
5 blanched almonds, toasted
25g (1oz) blackberries
500ml (18fl oz) good-quality vodka or brandy
50g (2oz) fresh sweet violet flowers,
    or 15g (¹/₁₆oz) dried
¼ vanilla pod
Piece of orange peel (about ⅛ orange)
10g (¼oz) fresh rose petals, or 2g (¹/₁₆oz) dried
200ml (7fl oz) Sweet violet syrup (see opposite)

Pound the toasted nuts to a paste and place in a jar with the blackberries. Add the vodka, cover and leave to infuse for 2 days. Add the violet flowers and vanilla pod and leave to infuse for another 2 days.

Add the piece of orange peel and rose petals and leave the mixture to infuse for 2 hours before straining through a coffee filter. Pour the flavoured alcohol into a freshly sterilized 700ml (1¼ pint) bottle and top up with the violet syrup. Store in a cupboard for up to a year; once opened, drink within 6 months. Serve neat over ice or in a cocktail.

Primrose
Primula vulgaris

Primroses are low-growing perennial herbs with five-petalled, butter-yellow flowers growing from rosettes of thick, tongue-shaped leaves. You'll find them everywhere, from dappled woodlands and stream embankments to gardens and even the edges of the busiest of roads. While primroses mainly flower in early to mid spring, in urban, sheltered spots you might find them blooming from midwinter onwards.

Primroses were once grown in monastic gardens as a medicinal herb; the flowers, leaves and roots turned into teas and infused in wine, traditionally used to reduce inflammation and pain, calm nerves and lift moods. With flowers that taste faintly of perfumed lemons and leaves that have hints of scented geranium, even the thought of eating sunshine-hued primrose flowers after a long, dark winter is surely enough to brighten the dullest of spirits.

Edible parts: Leaves and flowers. The roots are used medicinally, but are not sustainable to harvest.

Harvesting: Harvest in early to late spring, or from midwinter in sheltered spots. Using primroses for their medicinal properties has led the plant to becoming endangered in some areas. Foragers can be part of the solution by spreading and sowing the green seeds that form at the base of the flower, never uprooting the plant and only harvesting where there is an abundance of them. A sheltered garden is the perfect place to grow and gather the flowers.

Pairs with: Rhubarb, lemon, cream, apple blossom, apple, elderflower, pine, sorrel, violet and blackcurrant leaves.

Locations: Woodlands, gardens and verges in Europe, Asia, temperate regions of Africa and America.

Caution: Primroses are easy to identify when they are in flower or with seed pods but outside the flowering season they are easy to confuse with the very toxic foxglove, so only gather when the flowers or seed pods are there.

How to drink: primrose

Light and floral, without any bitterness, primrose flowers and leaves are best used in sweeter, fruity drinks.

 Wine: Traditional recipes for primrose wines rely on an abundance of flowers that is outside most people's reach today. If you only have a few handfuls, infuse them into a dessert wine to serve over ice.

 Cordials/syrups: With the addition of lemon juice, infuse primrose petals into sugar syrups to sweeten teas, cocktails and soft drinks.

 Ice cubes: Primrose flowers hold their beauty in floral ice cubes. Use boiled or distilled water to make clear ice cubes, placing half-made cubes in the freezer before covering with more water to encase the flowers.

 Tea: Fresh or dried, primrose leaves and flowers release their perfume in exquisite floral teas. Ideally suited to overnight cold infusion, the petals and leaves are lovely paired with apple blossom and grapefruit peel.

 Fermented drinks: Primrose leaves pair with nettles, pine needles and blackcurrant leaves to make delicious wild sodas.

 Vinegars: Infuse into apple cider vinegar or a light Champagne vinegar, with a sweetening of sugar or honey, to make a springtime drinking vinegar.

 Salts/sugars: Primrose flowers and leaves pounded up with sea salt make a fantastic finishing salt for cocktails. Pound freshly gathered petals or leaves into sugar, dehydrate (see page 234) and store to use later in the year.

Primrose & nettle water kefir

Primroses and nettles share a fresh, floral flavour
that is incredible in sour, fizzy water kefir drinks.
There are two simple fermentations: the first makes
the sour base of the drink and the second is when
flavours are added. You can use any blend of fruit,
herbs or flowers at this stage to create unique drinks.

MAKES 500ML (18FL OZ)

20g (³/₄oz) water kefir grains (if you have freshly
    bought grains you might need to reactivate
    them following your supplier's instructions)
500ml (18fl oz) unchlorinated water
2 tablespoons sugar (not honey, this would
    stop the fermentation)
10g (¹/₄oz) washed primrose flowers
20g (³/₄oz) washed primrose leaves
20g (³/₄oz) washed young nettle leaves

To make the base kefir drink, stir together the
water, kefir grains and 1 tablespoon of sugar in
a sterilized jar. Cover with a cloth and keep out
of direct sunlight in a place that's around 20°C
(68°F) for 2–4 days.

    When it starts to bubble, strain the grains (they
can be reused) and pour the liquid back into the
jar with the primrose flowers, primrose leaves and
nettle leaves. Press the flowers and leaves into the
liquid, cover and leave to infuse for 12 hours. Strain,
then pour the liquid into a bottle with a good seal
(a flip-top lid bottle is ideal) and, using a funnel,
add another tablespoon of sugar. Seal, shake and
leave for 3–5 days to carbonate.

    Water kefir will keep for a couple of weeks in
the fridge; it will keep fermenting so open the
lid every couple of days to release pressure.

Primrose, sorrel & elderflower sour

New primrose leaves keep their tender perfume
until early summer, offering a last hoorah just as
the first elderflowers start opening. Together with
sorrel and crab apple pectin, this alcohol-free
cocktail tastes and feels like all that is vibrant
and refreshing in late spring.

SERVES 2

20g (³/₄oz) primrose leaves
20g (³/₄oz) sorrel leaves
300ml (¹/₂ pint) crab apple pectin (see page 178)
    or sour apple juice
2 teaspoons elderflower cordial (see page 69)
Dash of bitters (such as the twig bitters on page 58)
Ice cubes
Apple blossom or primrose flowers, to decorate

Place the primrose leaves, sorrel, pectin and
cordial in a blender and process until the leaves
have broken up and the liquid turned a pale green.
Pass through a sieve and return the liquid to the
blender, blitzing again until it has a foamy top.

    Transfer to an ice-filled cocktail shaker (with a
shot or two of gin if you'd like this drink to be more
intoxicating than purifying), shake and strain into
two chilled coupe glasses. Add a dash of bitters,
according to taste. Decorate with apple blossom
or a late primrose flower and drink in the sunshine.

Magnolia
Magnolia spp.

Magnolias are ancient flowering trees that evolved long before flying pollinators like bees. Pollinated instead by beetles, the flowers have dense petals sturdy enough for insects to crawl around on. You'll often find different species of magnolia planted in residential gardens. In the wild they grow in areas as diverse as the South American rainforest and the mountainsides of Sichuan.

Across the world, the perfumed flowers, buds, barks and leaves have historically been used as flavourings for food and drink – nowhere perhaps more than in Mexico where the Aztec people used species such as the Mexican magnolia to flavour drinking chocolate. In China, magnolia's perfumed bark is used as a traditional Chinese medicine. The scented flowers are used to flavour oolong teas, made by fermenting the young tips of the tea plant on top of magnolia flowers, allowing the tea leaves to absorb the flowers' perfume as they ferment.

Edible parts: Twigs, bark, buds, flowers and leaves.

Harvesting: The flowers bruise easily, and a hard frost can wilt them overnight, turning them brown, but they can still be harvested and dried. The petals have a high water content and will need a couple of days in a dehydrator. Once dry, grind and store in an airtight container. Gather young leaves and bark in mid to late spring.

Pairs with: Ginger, cardamom, lemongrass, nutmeg, cinnamon, vanilla, rhubarb, pine, rosemary, lemon, honey, black tea, chocolate, sake, vermouth, white wine and gin.

Locations: Magnolias grow wild in America and Asia and are commonly found in gardens and parks around the world.

Caution: It is best to use the species with proven edibility, including: *M. denudata*, *M. kobus*, *M. mexicana*, *M.* x *soulangeana* and *M. grandiflora*.

How to drink: magnolia

Fresh magnolia petals range in flavour from ginger to cardamom and lemon – try out the different edible species to find your favourite. The leaves also have a range of flavours (warming spice or citrus) and the bark a perfumed cardamom note.

Wine: Dried or fresh magnolia flowers add a spiced honeyed sweetness to wines.

Liqueurs: Soak magnolia flowers in a neutral spirit and sugar for 24 hours. Add a sprinkle of citric acid to prevent the liqueur from browning, strain and bottle.

Cocktails: Magnolia flowers infused into syrups make delicious spritzers and gin cocktails.

Cordials/syrups: Magnolia syrup has a gingery floral flavour and is delicious when used to sweeten cocktails and teas.

Tea: Dried flowers, leaves and bark can be used in teas. Magnolia is lovely in the Uplifting spring tea on page 31.

Warming/milky drinks: Add a spoonful of dried magnolia flowers or a drizzle of syrup to hot chocolate and drink like the Aztecs. Spiced magnolia flowers and leaves are a great addition to chai teas. Pair them with cardamom, cinnamon and ginger, along with black tea leaves, to make a warming milky tea.

Fermented drinks: Magnolia flowers are delicious when fermented into wild sodas, or added to secondary fermentations of drinks like kombucha and ginger beer.

Vinegars: Magnolia flowers make a light, refreshing drinking vinegar.

Vin de magnolia

This recipe is perfect for those of us who don't have a whole tree to harvest from. This French fortified wine uses just a couple of magnolia flowers and turns a pocketful of petals into enough delicious aperitif for a feast.

———————

MAKES 1 LITRE (1³/₄ PINTS)
2 freshly opened magnolia flowers
100g (3¹/₂oz) sugar
1 vanilla pod, split lengthways
1 bottle of light red wine (such as a Pinot Noir)
250ml (9fl oz) eau de vie or brandy

Pull the magnolia petals from the flower, place them at the bottom of a wide-necked jar and cover with the sugar and the vanilla pod. Pour over the red wine and brandy and leave to infuse for 2 weeks, stirring each day and pushing any petals that rise to the surface under the liquid. If they keep coming to the top, use a clean fermenting weight to hold them down.

Strain the aperitif through a coffee filter into freshly sterilized bottles. This will keep for up to a month in the fridge but is best drunk fresh.

Magnolia & ginger beer

Magnolia petals are lovely ingredients in fermented drinks such as kombucha, kvass and wild sodas. Using a ginger bug starter will give a subtle flavour without overpowering the floral flavour of the magnolia petals. Magnolia ginger beer is delicious with a squeeze of lime or can be used as the mixer for a floral Moscow Mule.

———————

MAKES 2 LITRES (3¹/₂ PINTS)
2 litres (3¹/₂ pints) water
150g (5oz) sugar
50g (2oz) fresh magnolia petals
80ml (2³/₄fl oz) ginger bug starter (see page 244)

Place the water and sugar in a saucepan and bring to the boil, stirring, until all the sugar has dissolved. Remove from the heat and stir in the magnolia petals. Cover the pan and leave to infuse overnight.

Strain through a muslin-lined sieve into a bowl. Stir in the ginger bug before pouring the liquid into freshly sterilized bottles and putting the lids on.

After a couple of days, the liquid will start to produce bubbles. Once this happens, open the lids a couple of times a day to release pressure. According to how fast it is fermenting, it will be ready to drink after anything between 5 and 14 days, when the drink is effervescent. When it has reached its desired fizz, place it in the fridge and drink within 3–4 weeks.

Flowering currant
Ribes sanguineum

Found along roadsides and in garden planting, flowering currants are deciduous shrubs that grow up to 3m (10ft) tall with currant-shaped leaves. Unlike other currants, the leaves are downy on the undersides and on the stems. The leaves start to open early in the spring at the same time as racemes (clusters) of small, pink bell-shaped flowers varying from bright magenta to a far paler pink. Each individual flower has five outer petals and a second set of tiny white petals in the middle surrounding the stamens. Like other currants, flowering currants produce a crop of edible berries later in the summer but their fruit is bland, devoid of acidity and sweetness.

Both the leaves and flowers are strongly fragranced, smelling like a heady bouquet of sage, thyme, roses and blackcurrants. After the flowers have disappeared you can use the leaves to flavour gins, syrups and teas – but the prime moment for this plant is when the flowers first open. They are so full of flavour they could be mistaken for fruit, so delicious you will want to use them through the year. Dry the flowers and leaves and store in airtight jars or, even better, store a tub of freshly plucked flowers in the freezer to capture the scent for months to come.

Edible parts: Flowers and leaves; the fruit is edible but without much flavour.

Harvesting: Gather flowers when they have just opened, on warm days for the sweetest of flavours. The leaves can be gathered until they start changing colour in autumn. The edible, if somewhat bland, berries ripen in the summer.

Pairs with: Rhubarb, pine, juniper, sorrel, apple, mint, angelica, hawthorn leaves, fennel, nettle, lemon, orange, grapefruit, apple, gin, sparkling wine and brandy.

Locations: Flowering currants grow in fertile, sunny spots, growing wild across the west coast of America, and in gardens across temperate regions of the world.

How to drink: flowering currant

Some people find the taste of flowering currant unappealing, but for the rest of us, gather the flowers and leaves to use fresh or dry them for later in the year.

 Wine: Flowering currant flowers make delicious, almost herbal wines. They're low in tannins and acid so add a cup of black tea and orange juice to the floral blend.

 Tea: Fresh or dried, the leaves and flowers add a fruity sweetness to herbal teas; they are delicious in a spring tea blended with mint, nettle, hawthorn leaves and fennel.

 Liqueurs: The flowers can be infused in a matter of hours into vodka. Sweeten with sugar or light honey to create a lovely tipple.

 Fermented drinks: Add the leaves and flowers to second fermentations of kombuchas, or use them to make wild sodas or champagnes by themselves or with other botanicals such as spruce tips, lemon balm or mint.

 Cocktails: Smash the flowers with mint into sour spring Mojitos or a Tom Collins.

 Vinegars: The sweet perfume of flowering currant flowers and leaves pairs beautifully with sour drinking vinegars, made with either apple or wine vinegars and infused at room temperature for at least a week before straining and sweetening to your taste.

 Cordials/syrups: The fresh, vibrant flowers act like a floral fruit at a time of the year when fresh fruits and flowers are thin on the ground. Make a cordial, with lemon juice.

Flowering currant shrub (drinking vinegar)

American drinking vinegar shrubs were created as a way to preserve fruits in drinks and are usually made with a combination of fruit, sugar and vinegar. Pedants may claim a shrub can't be a shrub without all three of these, but the flavour of flowering currant is so fruity that even a purist would be fooled into believing they were drinking a fruit rather than a flower.

————————

MAKES 1 LITRE (1³/₄ PINTS)
400ml (14fl oz) boiling water
300g (10¹/₂oz) unrefined sugar
Pared zest of 1 orange
Pared zest of 1 lemon
100g (3¹/₂oz) flowering currant blossoms
250ml (9fl oz) cider vinegar

Place the water and sugar in a saucepan and bring to the boil, stirring, until the sugar dissolves.

Add the zest and remove from the heat before adding the blossoms, stirring to make sure the flowers are covered with syrup. Cover and leave for 24 hours.

Strain into a freshly sterilized jar, add the cider vinegar, seal and leave to mature. You can drink this straight away but traditionally shrubs are left to mature for a few months before drinking.

To drink, mix one part shrub with four parts sparkling water and serve over ice.

Uplifting spring tea

Flowering currant flowers are used in flower remedies for people who are feeling down-hearted at the end of winter. This delicious, fruity blend features other herbs that are thought to lift moods and they all happen to flower at the same time. Obviously, you don't need to feel blue to enjoy this cup of tea.

————————

MAKES 1 LITRE (1³/₄ PINTS)
20g (³/₄oz) flowering currant flowers and leaves
20g (³/₄oz) hawthorn leaves
20g (³/₄oz) magnolia petals
20g (³/₄oz) primrose petals and leaves
20g (³/₄oz) young nettle leaves
20g (³/₄oz) lemon balm or mint leaves

Dry the flowers and leaves in a dehydrator on a very low setting or in an airing cupboard (dry the magnolia separately as it will need longer to dehydrate). Crumble the dried ingredients into a bowl until the pieces are small but not powdery, then decant into an airtight 1 litre (1³/₄ pint) jar.

To serve, use a good pinch or 1 teaspoon of the mixture per person and infuse for 10 minutes in just-boiled water before straining.

Nettle
Urtica dioica

Nettles are perennial plants, growing in clumps, their roots spreading like ropes through the ground. Each spring, tender new growth appears so fast and full of flavour that early spring air becomes scented with the plant's minerally, sweet perfume. Look for the heart-shaped leaves that are lined with a serrated edge. These leaves grow around square stems and both the leaves and stems are covered in stinging hairs – once stung you are unlikely to forget what a nettle looks like.

Fortunately, the stinging hairs are neutralized by either pounding the plant or cooking it and nettles are one of the most nutritious plants around: rich in minerals such as calcium, vitamins including vitamin C, and protein. They also have a wide range of other health benefits, from supporting circulation to reducing inflammation and histamine responses. The sequin-like seeds are revered for their stress-reducing and kidney-supporting qualities and even the stings contain bone health-supporting silica.

Edible parts: Young leaves, seeds and roots (mainly used medicinally).

Harvesting: Use leaves from young plants before they grow flowers. They peak in the spring and early autumn, when there is a second flush of tender growth. Pick the seeds during the summer; take care as the leaf stings are at their most potent then.

Pairs with: Lemon, orange, rose, mint, fennel, pine, juniper, sloe and blackberry.

Locations: Nettles thrive in areas rich in nitrogen.

Caution: Only ever harvest nettles from ground that has not been contaminated; avoiding industrial areas, graveyards or near areas of busy, or standing, traffic. Only pick young nettle plants, before they have started to produce flower stems (older nettles can irritate your kidneys and bladder).

How to drink: nettle

According to how it is used and how long it is soaked for, nettle can provide anything from a deep umami flavour to a light, floral, delicate rose-like flavour. Treat nettles like flowers and only infuse the leaves for a short time in water or alcohol for the best taste.

 Wine: Nettles make a light, almost floral wine. Add citrus fruits for acidity, and a cup of black or blackberry leaf tea for tannins. Unlike a lot of wines, nettle wine is best drunk young, once the fermentation has stopped (usually around 12 weeks).

 Beer: Grain-free nettle beer is herbal, lightly alcoholic and quick to make.

 Spirits: Nettle leaves infuse their flavours and colour remarkably quickly into spirits. Pack washed nettles into a wide-necked jar and cover with a juniper-strong gin (such as a London dry gin).

 Cordials/syrups: Nettle cordial is vibrant and fruity; adding lemon or grapefruit juice turns the cordial bright pink. Try adding young spruce, Douglas fir tips or blackcurrant leaves.

 Tea: Nettle leaves and seeds make delicious herbal teas. Cold-infused nettle tea soaked overnight tastes light and floral, but the process will not remove the sting so make sure you strain any leaves from your drink before consuming.

 Fermented drinks: Dilute nettle cordial and pour into a plastic bottle. Within a few days it will start to ferment, providing a health-supporting probiotic drink full of minerals and vitamins. Cold nettle infusions are delicious turned into water kefir drinks, like Primrose & nettle water kefir on page 23).

Nettle small beer

My grandmother-in-law hailed from a tiny village in South Wales where the miners' wives would make small beer for their soot-covered husbands. Full of nettles, cleavers, blackcurrant leaves and dandelions, it provided much-needed fortification.

————

MAKES 2.25 LITRES (4 PINTS)
120g (4oz) nettle leaves
60g (2oz) mixed dandelion, cleavers and
   blackcurrant leaves
2 litres (3½ pints) water
200g (7oz) sugar
Juice of 2 lemons
Pinch of brewer's yeast

Place all the leaves in a large bowl of cold water, use a spoon to stir them and loosen any debris, then drain into a colander. Heat the water in a large saucepan to a simmer, drop in the leaves and cook for 10 minutes. Remove the leaves with a slotted spoon, then add the sugar to the pan and stir until dissolved. Allow to cool, then stir in the lemon juice and yeast. Cover and leave somewhere warm for 12 hours, or until the yeast starts working and bubbles form.

Pass the liquid through a sieve lined with fine muslin to get rid of any remaining pieces of leaf, then transfer to a freshly sterilized demijohn. Ferment for 1 week before transferring to plastic bottles.

Keep the bottles at room temperature and loosen the lids a couple of times a day to allow excess pressure to escape. The beer is ready to drink a week after bottling. It can be left for longer but be warned, it will become more and more alcoholic.

Nettle cordial

Nettle cordial is a drink all children and adults should not only drink, but also make. Nettles are pH indicators so when acid is added to the brew, the liquid turns pink. Not only is the drink pink, it's also utterly delicious and makes the most incredible nettle Gimlets (not for children though).

————

MAKES 1.5 LITRES (2¾ PINTS)
60g (2oz) young nettle tips
1 litre (1¾ pints) water
1kg (2lb 4oz) sugar
Juice of 6 lemons

Place the leaves in a large bowl of cold water, use a spoon to stir them and loosen any debris, then drain into a colander.

Meanwhile, bring the water to the boil in a large saucepan, turn off the heat and plunge the nettles into the water, pressing them down to ensure they are fully submerged. Leave them to soak for 30 minutes, then remove the leaves (you can use them in soups). Pour the nettle-infused water through a sieve lined with a double layer of muslin into another pan, place on the heat and, when simmering, stir in the sugar until it is completely dissolved. Turn off the heat and leave for 10 minutes before adding the lemon juice, pouring it through the muslin to catch any pieces of lemon.

The cordial should be pink – if not, add more lemon juice as the pink colour indicates acidity, which helps preserve the drink. Pour into freshly sterilized bottles and keep in the fridge for up to a month. Pasteurized cordial (see page 235) will keep up to 12 months.

Ground ivy
Glechoma hederacea

Ground ivy is a member of the mint family which, as well as being home to menthol mints, also comprises sage, rosemary and catnip. Ground ivy sits (or crawls) right in the middle of their flavour profiles – earthy, herbal and bitter with the faintest hint of mint. You might know this plant by its other names of creeping Jenny, creeping Charlie or runaway Robin – all names that rather aptly describe one of its key traits: how it creeps across the ground. While these names give an indication of how the plant grows, another name it's known by gives a hint at how it can be drunk: ale hoof.

The word 'hoof' comes from the old English for ivy, and 'ale' – well, you can probably guess what that refers to. Ground ivy has a long (and trailing) history of being used to brew ale, helping to flavour, clarify and preserve the drink before hops took over. When ground ivy was the herb of choice in ale making, ale was weak, full of other herbs and often safer to drink than water. This kind of ale was known as 'gruit' and ground ivy was often paired with herbs like yarrow, heather, horehound, mugwort and sweet gale, making a brew that packed a medicinal punch as well as a unique flavour.

Edible parts: Flowers, stems and leaves.

Harvesting: You can harvest ground ivy all year but it's easiest to find in the summer and autumn when trails of heart-shaped leaves with scalloped edges can be found at the bases of hedges and shrubs. However, it is most delicious in the spring when the new growth hasn't yet flopped and the plant has its little lavender-blue flowers.

Pairs with: Honey, lemon, liquorice, spices, yarrow, mint, sage, pine, heather, molasses, chocolate, horseradish and nettle.

Locations: Under hedges and shrubs. Ground ivy likes shady, damp ground.

How to drink: ground ivy

Ground ivy can be used fresh or dried. Cooking or drying mellows the raw flavours, turning them more savoury, earthy and less minty.

Beer: Add ground ivy to herbal home brewing to make traditional-style ales.

Cocktails: Ground ivy is delicious added to a Bloody Mary, an Old Fashioned or a Mojito.

Cordials/syrups: Ground ivy syrup is a traditional herbal medicine for ear, nose and throat conditions, but is also used to flavour drinks.

Tea: Ground ivy has a long association with a herbal tea known as gill tea, where it is paired with liquorice root. Ground ivy tea is also lovely with honey and lemon.

Warming/milky drinks: Add powdered ground ivy and nettles to cocoa powder to make deeply flavoured herbal hot chocolates.

Fermented drinks: Add dried ground ivy to ginger beers and kombuchas for a herbal kick.

Ground ivy iced tea

Ground ivy tea is traditionally served chilled with lemon and honey, making it one step away from the ultimate cold tea – iced tea.

————————

MAKES 1 LITRE (1³/₄ PINTS)
4 teaspoons dried black tea
2 tablespoons unrefined sugar
1 tablespoon light honey
1 litre (1³/₄ pints) boiling water
10g (¹/₄oz) bowl full of fresh ground ivy
Ice cubes
Juice of 1 lemon
1 lemon, sliced
1 orange, sliced
10g (¹/₄oz) fresh mint leaves

Place the tea, sugar and honey in a jug and cover with the just-boiled water. Stir to dissolve the honey and sugar and leave to brew for 10 minutes before straining.

Add half the ground ivy to the tea and let the brew cool. When cold, strain and discard the ground ivy.

Fill a jug with ice and add the lemon juice, fruit slices, mint and remaining ground ivy. Pour over the cooled tea, stir and serve in ice-filled glasses, adding extra honey if desired to sweeten and a ground ivy flower stem to decorate.

Ground ivy & liquorice ale

Ground ivy and liquorice combine together to make this make a delicious, quick-to-ferment low-alcohol ale. You can use fresh or dried ground ivy in this recipe, which is useful because it is especially delicious in the colder months when snow might be covering your trailing herbs.

————————

MAKES 5 LITRES (9 PINTS)
4 litres (7 pints) water
40g (1¹/₂oz) liquorice root
50g (2oz) fresh ground ivy, or 20g (³/₄oz) dried
450g (1lb) malt extract
225g (8oz) brown sugar, plus extra for bottling
150g (5oz) honey
10g (¹/₄oz) brewer's yeast

Place the water in a large saucepan and bring to the boil. Add the liquorice root and simmer for 1 hour. Remove from the heat, add half the ground ivy and let the brew cool to 71°C (160°F) before stirring in the malt extract, sugar, honey and remaining ground ivy. Cool the brew to 21°C (70°F), then stir in the yeast.

Pour the ale into a freshly sterilized fermenting vessel and leave for 7–10 days until specks of foam start to form on the top. Transfer to sturdy sterilized bottles, adding 1 teaspoon of sugar to each bottle, and leave for another 7–10 days before drinking. This ale is best drunk fresh.

Scots pine
Pinus sylvestris

Despite its name implying otherwise, the Scots pine is globally the most widely spread species of pine tree, found everywhere from the Arctic to the south of Spain. The slender trunks are covered with scaly red bark and they grow up to 45m (148ft) in height, topped with a mop of twisted branches covered in pairs of long evergreen needles. You'll often find trees with lower-hanging branches, which is lucky because Scots pine is made up of edible, nutritious and delicious parts.

While its evergreen needles are a year-round harvest, in the spring it produces three of the most sought-after pine crops. First are the buds – sticky, resinous and lemon-flavoured. These are used to make teas and flavour liqueurs, sodas and syrups. Next comes the powdery yellow pollen, formed inside the flowers. This is harvested as a food supplement, revered as a stimulant and hormone balancer. Last are the cones which, for the first year, are green and tender enough to release their resinous flavour. These can be turned into syrups or preserved whole to use as a garnish.

Edible parts: New shoots, cones, needles, bark, pollen and resin.

Harvesting: Look for a young tree or one with low-hanging branches. To help identify the tree, look at its tough long needles: you'll see that they grow in pairs – different species have different numbers of needles in each cluster; others, like white pine, have five. The buds, shoots and pollen can be harvested in spring, the green cones in summer and the needles, bark and resin all year.

Pairs with: Rhubarb, flowering currant, mint, nettle, blackcurrant, lemon, grapefruit, gin, molasses, rum and whisky.

Locations: Forests, hillsides and parks.

Caution: Don't use pine pollen if you have a pollen allergy. Avoid using if pregnant. If you don't have access to Scots pine, some other species are edible, but not all. Make sure to identify your species before harvesting.

How to drink: Scots pine

The vibrant citrus flavour of young Scots pine needles and buds changes as they age. Older needles have a more warming, woody, rosemary flavour that is no less delicious, just different, and will need to infuse for longer to extract their flavour.

Beer: Like other edible evergreen trees, pine needles, cones and even bark can be used in beer. Spruce tip beer on page 217 can be made with pine needles instead.

Liqueurs: All edible parts make great liqueurs and release their flavours very quickly, so taste after a few hours of infusing. Over-infusing will make an incredibly strong flavouring, only suitable for using in bitters or tinctures.

Cordials/syrups: The needles and cones of pine trees create very different types of syrups. The needles have a floral, vanilla flavour and are best infused into white sugar, while the resinous cones have a deeper flavour, more suited to soaking in brown sugar to allow the natural liquids to absorb into it.

Tea: Pine needles and new buds are delicious in tea. Pick and dry the new buds to use throughout the year – they are lovely paired with floral flavours such as primrose, elderflower or rose.

Fermented drinks: Pine cones and needles have a coating of natural yeasts and make delicious naturally carbonated drinks. You can use pine cones to add yeast to ferment other drinks – they're lovely added to fruit sodas such as strawberry, rhubarb or apple.

Vinegars: Pack pine needles or cones into a jar, add a teaspoon of live cider vinegar and cover with water to start fermenting a tasty, vitamin-C-rich vinegar which can be sweetened and drunk as a cordial or used to add sourness to cocktails.

Bitters/tinctures: Cram a small jar with pine needles, cones, bark or resin, and cover with a high-proof neutral spirit. Leave to infuse for a few months, then strain and bottle into an amber dropper bottle. A drop of the extract will add incredible pine flavour without overwhelming a drink. Pine bark extract is used as a herbal supplement.

Pine needle soda

The natural yeasts and lemon flavours in pine needles make them a perfect ingredient in delicious fizzy drinks. The result is sweet, lemony and uncannily similar to shop-bought pops but far healthier as it's full of probiotics and vitamins.

_____

MAKES 750ML (1 PINT 7FL OZ)
4 tablespoons white sugar
60g (2oz) pine needles
Filtered, unchlorinated water, to top

Sterilize a 1 litre (1³/₄ pint) jar, add the sugar and pine needles and top up with the water, making sure the needles are all under the liquid.

Tightly seal the jar with a sterilized lid and shake to dissolve the sugar. Place the jar in a warm room away from direct sunlight for 3 days, each day turning the jar to make sure the needles are all soaking. After 3 days, open the lid. If there is a fizz, the drink is ready to serve (it may need longer to ferment in colder temperatures). Serve with ice and a slice of lemon.

Pine cone syrup

While this syrup was traditionally used as an antiviral immune booster, it's more in demand now in a cocktail. Try adding a little to an Old Fashioned or a Martini, or make a hot toddy by adding a spoonful to a mug of hot water along with a slice of ginger and a dash of rum. Select cones that are green and in their first year. If using very small cones you might need to add a little water. This is a slow recipe, taking weeks of patience but you'll be rewarded with a rich syrup.

_____

MAKES ABOUT 200ML (7FL OZ)
200g (7oz) young pine cones
200g (7oz) light muscovado sugar

Wash the pine cones and place them in a large bowl, sprinkle over the sugar and stir well. Pack the mixture into a sterilized jar, topping with more sugar if necessary to make sure the cones are covered. Seal and leave to macerate in direct sunlight. The yeasts in the pine cones will start to create a fermentation – this is perfectly normal. Every few days, open the jar and give the pine cones a stir – you might need to add more sugar if the cones are not completely covered.

After about a month, the pine cones will have released all their liquid and the sugar will have turned into a dark syrup. Spoon the contents of the jar into a saucepan and bring to a simmer for a minute before straining the syrup into a sterilized bottle. Store in the fridge for up to 6 months. If the strained cones are small and soft, you can eat them or add to drinks.

Gorse
Ulex spp.

Gorse are dense, spiky bushes that grow in swathes across sand dunes and heathland. Their needle-like leaves cover the plant all year and are often accompanied by a smattering of bright yellow flowers that produce seeds encased in shells just like pea pods (gorse is a member of the pea or Fabaceae family). It's not the seeds of gorse you want to eat, but the flowers, which on warm days emanate a perfume that smells and tastes of coconut. There's an old proverb that says that gorse is in flower except when kissing is out of style – which of course it never is. Sometimes there will just be a few flowers, but in the spring they are abundant, turning shorelines and hillsides bright yellow.

Head out to a sand dune or a hillside on a warm spring day with some gloves and you'll be able to harvest plenty of flowers – just make sure you stand on the sunny side of the shrub, because when the sun hits the flowers, they taste of honeyed, earthy coconut. The flowers on the cooler side of the shrub give away the pea family flavours.

Edible parts: Flowers (not seeds), needle-like leaves and branches, used for infusing.

Harvesting: Harvest in the morning on warm, sunny days. Pick flowers from the side of the shrub in full sun for the strongest coconut flavour and discard the bitter hairy shell the flower sits in.

Pairs with: Blackberry buds, chocolate, vanilla, cinnamon, rum, whiskey, orange, lemon, lime, pineapple, coconut and almond.

Locations: Coastal dunes and inland heathland.

Caution: Don't gorge on gorse – the flowers contain an alkaloid that is harmful in large quantities. Take care not to confuse gorse with inedible flowers such as the very toxic laburnum.

How to drink: gorse

As much as gorse flowers smell most fragrant when they're in warm sun, too much heat when cooking dissipates their flavour. Infuse freshly gathered flowers in warm syrups rather than hot.

Wine: Gorse flowers make a rich coconut-flavoured wine. Use lemons to add acidity.

Spirits: Gorse is often added to botanical gins, including Isle of Bute gin, which puts gorse as its main flavour along with juniper. In Ireland, there is a long tradition of infusing whiskey with gorse flowers, to give the drink a golden colour and a distinctive flavour.

Cordials/syrups: Gorse flower cordial is delicious in soft and alcoholic drinks alike. To capture the best flavour, make a citrus-infused sugar syrup with limes, oranges or lemons and pour the warm syrup over the gorse petals; stir and leave to infuse overnight before decanting.

Tea: Gorse flower tea is drunk in Europe and South America. In Brazil, the flowers (known as carqueja) are drunk as a liver-supporting tea to help with hangovers.

Gorse flower rum

Gorse flowers are delicious infused into rum. So are limes and vanilla and, fortunately, the four ingredients work beautifully together to make a rum as warm and fragrant as the sunny side of a gorse bush.

MAKES 500ML (18FL OZ)
500ml (18fl oz) white rum
30g (1oz) gorse flowers
Pared zest of $1/4$ lime
$1/4$ vanilla pod
2 teaspoons unrefined sugar

If you can, take a wide-necked jar filled with the rum with you when harvesting and place your flowers straight into it. Otherwise, put the flowers in the spirit as soon as you can. Add the zest, vanilla and sugar and stir to dissolve. Cover it with a disc of baking paper to stop the flowers from floating and leave to infuse for 2 days.

Strain the rum into a sterilized bottle and drink within about 3 months. Gorse flower rum makes a quite wonderful Daiquiri. Simply shake 1 tablespoon of lime juice with 50ml (2fl oz) of the infused rum, 2 teaspoons of simple sugar syrup and some ice cubes and strain into a chilled glass.

Gorse Old Fashioned

Adding gorse flower syrup to an Old Fashioned cocktail is proof that Irish whiskey makers knew a thing or two when they added gorse to their spirits. Warming and nutty, it's the perfect tipple after a prickly day gorse harvesting.

SERVES 2
75g (3oz) sugar
100ml ($3^1/2$fl oz) water
50g (2oz) gorse flowers
Pared zest of $1/2$ unwaxed orange
2 large ice cubes
120ml (4fl oz) Irish whiskey
Soda water (optional)

To make a gorse flower syrup, place the sugar and water in a saucepan and bring to a simmer, stirring, until the sugar has dissolved. Take off the heat and leave until the syrup is just warm, then stir in the gorse flowers and orange zest. Cover and leave to infuse overnight.

Strain the syrup into a sterilized bottle and keep in the fridge for up to 2 weeks. To make an Old Fashioned, place a large ice cube in each of two glasses and top each with 2 teaspoons of the gorse syrup. Divide the whiskey between the glasses, stir with a cocktail spoon and serve. You can top up with soda water if you like a longer drink.

Sorrel
Rumex acetosa

The name sorrel originates from the Anglo-German word *sur*, meaning sour – and these plants really do live up to their name. Of all the sour-tasting sorrels, common sorrel is the kind you're most likely to have a chance to harvest because, as its name indicates, it's an incredibly common plant, growing often unnoticed in lawns and through grasslands. Its little hairless leaves are shaped like rounded arrowheads, with tips that look like pointed shirt collars. Sorrel grows in clumps and when there's one sorrel plant, you'll usually find you're surrounded by them.

During the summer, sorrel plants growing in uncut areas divert their energy from leaves to growing wispy flower stems. The stems are topped with little delicate pink flowers; these turn into papery seeds that look like they are balancing on the tips of the flowering stems. Come the early autumn, the plant will be rejuvenated in its flavour, with fresh, sour leaves to harvest right through until next summer. When at its peak, sorrel adds a vibrant, refreshing tang, with flavours of lemon, lime and apple.

Edible parts: The leaves, stems, flowers and seeds.

Harvesting: Sorrel leaves range in size from micro herbs to large floppy leaves. The older ones are more astringent. Pick them in early to late spring, or in late summer to late autumn (through winter in mild locations). The summer flowers and seeds are also edible, with a mild, astringent taste and powdery texture.

Pairs with: Rhubarb, magnolia, mint, apple, lemon, kiwi, elderflower, rose, primrose, pine, spruce, nettle, gin and tequila.

Locations: Meadows and grasslands, including garden lawns.

Caution: Sorrel is rich in oxalic acid and people who have kidney conditions need to limit their intake of foods with high levels of it. Sorrel looks very similar and grows in similar locations to the toxic arum lily (*Arum maculatum*). Arum lily leaves have curved tips and a more crazed, silvery back, but is still easy to confuse the two plants.

How to drink: sorrel

Nutritious and vibrant tasting, blending the leaves in apple juice or water will create a bright green, fresh ingredient for sour drinks.

Liqueurs: A number of craft gin distillers include sorrel in their botanicals, adding a fresh, citrus, grassy flavour to the drinks. Infusing leaves for 24 hours in gin or vodka will extract the flavour into the spirit. Sorrel-infused syrup blended with spirits makes a sweet, tangy liqueur.

Cordials/syrups: Sorrel syrup is best made by blending the fresh leaves with a cooled sugar syrup. Make in small batches to use fresh or freeze until needed to prevent the cordial from discolouring – don't worry if it does lose colour, it will still taste delicious even if it's not as beautiful.

Tea: Sorrel leaves add a lemony tang to herbal teas. Try pairing them with elderflower, fennel and nettles.

Fermented drinks: Sorrel's sour tang is delicious in fermented drinks. Add a handful of chopped leaves to apple juice with a ginger bug or cider vinegar starter, or add the leaves to kvass-style and sima drinks (see page 243).

Vinegars: Soak sorrel leaves in apple cider vinegar for a few days before straining and sweetening with honey or sugar to make a delicious doubly sour drinking vinegar.

Rhubarb & sorrel granita gimlet

Sorrel and rhubarb are perfect partners in gin-based drinks. Served as a granita, the vibrant green colour makes a beautiful contrast to the pink rhubarb. The granita is lovely in a wide range of drinks and freezes well so it is worth making in bulk if you have a large amount to harvest.

SERVES 2

75g (2¹/₂oz) granulated sugar
150ml (5fl oz) water
100g (3¹/₂oz) sorrel, roughly chopped,
    plus extra to decorate
Juice of ¹/₂ lime
Pinch of salt
200g (7oz) rhubarb, chopped
Ice cubes
120ml (4fl oz) gin

Place the sugar and water in a saucepan and heat. Stir until the sugar has dissolved then leave to cool. Pour 100ml (3¹/₂fl oz) of the syrup into a blender, add the sorrel and blend until smooth. Pass through a sieve into a plastic tub and stir in the lime juice and salt. Place in the freezer and leave to harden. When solid, use a knife to scrape the granita into shavings. Keep in the freezer until needed.

Put the rhubarb in a saucepan over a medium heat with 150ml (5fl oz) water and gently cook until it has softened, then strain the juice.

Fill a cocktail shaker with ice and add 100ml (3¹/₂fl oz) of the remaining sugar syrup, 100ml (3¹/₂fl oz) of the rhubarb juice and the gin. Shake and divide between two chilled cocktail glasses, filling them only halfway. Remove the granita from the freezer and pile it into the glasses. Top with a sorrel leaf and serve immediately.

Sorrel smoothie with kiwi & apple

Sorrel is packed full of minerals and vitamins – 100g (3¹/₂oz) of fresh sorrel contains an astounding 80 per cent of your daily vitamin C needs. With the addition of fruit and yogurt, sorrel smoothies are a great way to add loads of nutrition in a way that even fussy children will like.

SERVES 2

40g (1¹/₂oz) sorrel leaves, rinsed
2 kiwis, peeled
1 banana, peeled
1 apple, cored and chopped
150g (5oz) yogurt

Place all the ingredients in a blender or smoothie maker and blend until smooth. Divide between two glasses and drink your vitamins.

Elm
Ulmus spp.

Elm trees are often found in overgrown hedgerows or the understorey of dappled woodland, their long branches lined with alternating oval, serrated leaves. During early spring, they produce clusters of tiny red flowers on thin stems. These mature into one of the finest, most ephemeral treats of spring – little green papery discs known as samaras, which encase the forming seeds. Harvest when pale green and you'll have a treat that tastes like a cross between a floral cucumber and a mild nut.

The bark of the native American elm, slippery elm (*Ulmus rubra*), has a long history of being harvested for its healing properties. Dried and ground to a powder, it is often added to drinks used during convalescence and for those who require drinks to be thickened. It's also useful for providing mouthfeel in cocktails, especially those made with cask-aged drinks with woody flavours or syrups made from tree saps such as maple or birch.

Edible parts: Seeds, bark, leaves and sap.

Harvesting: Look up at an elm in spring and you'll see long branches covered with pale green clusters of seeds, rounded with a seed in the centre. The most common part to use is the inner bark, harvested in spring; peel away the gnarly outer bark to reveal it. It is dried for use through the year.

Pairs with: Samaras with linden, apple, elderflower, mint, cleavers, fennel and hawthorn; inner bark with malt, milk, maple syrup, cardamom, vanilla and whisky.

Locations: Northern hemisphere woodland, overgrown hedgerows, town streets and parks globally.

Note: Over-harvesting causes damage so only take from fallen branches or trees that have been felled. In America, Siberian elm (*U. pumila*) is an invasive species and is more sustainable than slippery elm. If you buy slippery elm bark powder, make sure it is from an approved sustainable source.

How to drink: elm

While elm seeds have a floral, refreshing perfume, elm bark is more woody with a slight sweetness like maple syrup. The bark tends to work best with richer-flavoured drinks than the seeds.

Liqueurs: Infuse the fresh seeds into a neutral spirit and sweeten with a small amount of light honey or white sugar to make a delicate, floral spring liqueur. Infusing the seeds into wine makes a delicious light aperitif – try replacing the thyme with elm seeds in the recipe for Thyme aperitif (see page 133).

Thickeners: You can use whole pieces of inner bark or powder. Pour cold water over the bark and leave for a couple of hours (overnight if you are using whole bark) to allow the mucilage to be absorbed into the liquid. If using the powder, mix it to a smooth paste first before diluting into your drink and sieve before serving to remove any grainy solids. Add sparingly – a little goes a long way. Slippery elm powder is often added to nourishing smoothies and its flavour works especially well with banana or strawberry.

Tea: The bark, seeds and leaves are all used to make healing teas. The bark is the best thickener and is traditionally used to heal gut inflammation. Use up to ½ teaspoon of powdered bark or a 5cm (2in) piece of whole bark. The leaves and samaras will give a fresher flavour, ideally paired with other spring leaves and flowers such as hawthorn leaves, nettles or mint.

Warming/milky drinks: Finely powdered elm bark is added to warm milky drinks with malted barley powder. To make homemade malt drinks, try adding vanilla or cocoa powder.

Fermented drinks: Add elm samaras to pine needle sodas or nettle beers for refreshing spring sparkling drinks.

Elm bark malted drink

Malted barley, like slippery elm, is rich in nutrition. And like slippery elm, it makes a restorative, easy-to-digest drink. Should you not want to use dairy milk powder, oat milk powder makes a great replacement. Powdered dried inner elm bark is sold as slippery elm bark if you wish to buy some.

MAKES 12 SERVINGS

1 tablespoon powdered dried inner elm bark
6 tablespoons barley malt powder
125g (4¹/₂oz) milk powder
1 tablespoon caster sugar
1 teaspoon ground cardamom or cinnamon
   (optional)

Sieve all the ingredients into a bowl, and mix together to make sure they are all thoroughly combined. Spoon into an airtight jar and store for up to 2 months.

To make the drink, place 2 heaped tablespoons of the powder in a mug and stir in 2 tablespoons of warm water to make a smooth paste. Top the mug up with hot water and stir until creamy. Serve hot or cold.

Elm seed fizz

Elm seeds and linden flowers both share the same soothing properties and beautiful floral fresh flavours, combining here to make a delicious drink of the woods. For those wanting to make a more boozy beverage, a measure of light gin is a rather lovely addition.

SERVES 2

30g (1oz) fresh elm samaras
1 teaspoon linden flower tea
200ml (7fl oz) water
Ice cubes
Juice of ¹/₂ lemon
15ml (¹/₂fl oz) sugar syrup or linden cordial
300ml (¹/₂ pint) soda water

Remove any stalks from the elm samaras and place them on a chopping board, reserving a few for decoration. Crush the samaras with a rolling pin to release the delicate flavours and immediately place them in a jug and cover with the water. Press the samaras and linden flower tea under the liquid and leave to infuse for 30 minutes.

Half-fill a cocktail shaker with ice. Strain the infused liquid through a sieve into the cocktail shaker and add the lemon juice and syrup. Shake for 30 seconds, then strain the drink into two coupes and top up with ice-cold soda water. Serve decorated with a few samaras.

Beech
Fagus spp.

Beech trees are among the most majestic in woodlands, parks and gardens. If growing in dense woodland, they will grow tall, high out of reach in the canopy. But if they have space to spread, they grow as wide as they are tall, with smooth grey bark and arching branches that can skim forest floors, providing easy harvest of their oval, pointed-tip leaves and spiny husk-encased nuts known as beech mast. When the nuts are ripe, the outer shell opens revealing small, triangular, oil-rich nuts. Once shelled, they can be roasted and ground into a coffee substitute similar to acorn coffee (see page 258) or infused into nut liqueurs.

The leaves on the tree start turning brown in autumn but often hold on until the next spring when the new leaves emerge. Rub a beech leaf and you'll notice it smells tannic and almost sweet, a bit like black tea – and dried brown beech leaves make a very delicious herbal drink, perhaps the closest thing to camellia tea. But the tender, newly opened, almost translucent spring leaves taste citrusy, oily and quite moreish.

Edible parts: Leaves, twigs, nuts and sap (sap is hard to collect in any volume).

Harvesting: New leaves are at their most flavoursome for the first few weeks of growth. Collect them while they are still tender, before the tannins build up. In late summer, gather the nuts from low branches when some have opened and fallen. If you collect unopened husks, store in a warm place and they will open as they ripen. Pick brown leaves from the tree on dry days.

Pairs with: Young leaves with larch, spruce tips, blackberry leaves, violet, lemon, sorrel, apple, rhubarb, gin and brandy; older brown leaves with rum, toffee and spices.

Locations: Beech grows in most temperate global regions, thriving in areas with damp but well-drained soil.

Note: Copper beech has dark purple leaves and masts, which are also edible.

How to drink: beech

Young beech leaves have an almost citrus flavour, tasting more like black tea as they brown and age. Beech nuts have a mild, oily, nutty flavour – they need roasting or boiling to drink (or eat) in any quantity.

Spirits: Infusing the leaves in spirits brings out their herbal, nutty flavours. Beech leaf noyau is made with a combination of gin and brandy (see opposite). The nuts make a delicious liqueur. Like walnut, beech can be paired with hazelnut in drinks similar to Nocello (see page 107). Sweeten beech nut liqueur with maple syrup for a true woody flavour.

Cocktails: For a few weeks in spring, the sweetly sour leaves can be blended with water and a sprinkling of sugar or a drop of violet syrup to make a sensational non-alcoholic sour cocktail. Purée beech leaves with spruce tips, apple juice and a dash of birch bitters in a blender to make a chlorophyll-green, non-alcoholic drink that tastes of woodlands in spring.

Cordials/syrups: Beech is one of the many tree species that produce an edible sap which, when reduced, makes a fruity, raisin- and plum-flavoured syrup (in tiny amounts).

Tea: Young freshly opened beech leaves are ambrosial in spring teas, especially blended with blackberry leaves. The papery browned leaves hold a black tea-like taste and make a perfectly respectable infused tea on their own, or can be blended with cinnamon, allspice and nutmeg for a warming chai-style decoction tea.

Coffee: Roasted beech nuts make a delicious nutty coffee substitute.

Milks: Boil ground-up beech masts in water and leave overnight before straining to make a creamy nut milk.

Bitters/tinctures: Browned beech leaves, paired with birch and oak, make a warming, woody bitter. Cover equal quantities of twigs and leaves from beech, birch and oak trees with a spirit such as rum, vodka or brandy. Let it infuse for a couple of months before decanting into dropper bottles.

Beech leaf noyau

This liqueur is made by soaking young beech leaves in gin, brandy and sugar. Noyaus hail from northern France and were originally made by infusing apricot, cherry kernels or even blackthorn leaves into a spirit such as Cognac. It also became a legendary tipple among the woodworkers of the Chiltern Hills in southern England.

MAKES 850ML (1¹/₂ PINTS)
150g (5oz) young beech leaves
500ml (18fl oz) gin
300g (10¹/₂oz) granulated sugar
250ml (9fl oz) water
100ml (3¹/₂fl oz) brandy

Press the leaves into a 1 litre (1³/₄ pint) glass jar until almost full, then slowly pour the gin over the leaves, allowing time for it to trickle to the bottom of the jar, filling it to the top and ensuring the leaves are completely submerged (you can use a piece of baking paper to press them down).

Leave to steep in a dark place for at least 2 weeks before straining through a fine sieve into a freshly sterilized bottle. You can leave them to infuse for months to create a woody, tannic drink; if you leave the leaves for only a couple of weeks the drink will be fresher, more herbal tasting.

Heat the sugar and water in a saucepan until the sugar has dissolved, allow to cool then add the brandy. Slowly add the mixture to the gin, tasting for your level of desired sweetness as you go. The noyau can be drunk immediately but, like all good things, improves with age and is delicious after a few months – in time for autumnal drinking.

Brown beech leaf & toffee rum

Beech leaves often cling onto the tips of branches until after the new year's growth has opened up. The brown, tea-flavoured leaves not only make a comforting brew, they also turn into a delicious tipple to warm cold spring or winter evenings (if it lasts that long).

MAKES 500ML (18FL OZ)
50g (2oz) brown beech leaves
75g (2¹/₂oz) toffee, cinder toffee or fudge
400ml (14fl oz) dark rum

Place the leaves in a 500ml (18fl oz) jar, followed by the toffee, using the sweets to weigh the leaves down. Pour over the dark rum to fill the jar, making sure that all the leaves are submerged (if they are not, place a piece of baking paper on top to stop the leaves rising above it). Seal and place the jar somewhere warm. Shake each day to help dissolve the toffee. Leave to infuse for 4 weeks before straining and bottling. Serve neat or like a woodland twist on hot buttered rum (drunk around a cosy beechwood fire for maximum effect).

Sweet woodruff
Galium odoratum

If you think there's something similar between the illustrations of sweet woodruff and cleavers on page 218, you'd be right – the two little plants belong to the same family, Rubiaceae. But while cleavers grow metres long with bristly edges and almost imperceptible flowers along the stem, sweet woodruff stays small, growing no more than 15–20cm (6–8in), with glossy, smooth and straight stems, topped with dainty white flowers at the tips. What it lacks in height, sweet woodruff makes up for in another way: when you harvest and dry the tiny plant, it fills the kitchen with the most incredible aroma – vanilla, almonds, earth – the scent of coumarin.

Coumarin is a chemical present in a lot of our favourite smells and flavours – from drying hay to vanilla, chamomile and even cinnamon – and sweet woodruff is one of the most rich in its beautiful flavours, tasting like vanilla, coconut and almonds all rolled into one. Gathering just before the flowers open in mid spring ensures its best flavour, one that is so highly regarded in Germany that you'd be hard pressed not to be offered a sweet woodruff drink in early May. Beers, wines and soft drinks all come with a seasoning of the little plant with a big flavour.

Edible parts: Leaves, stems and flowers.

Harvesting: Gather sweet woodruff from spring until autumn, but it is at its peak in spring just before the flowers open. Snip the top half of the plants rather than pulling up the whole plant to allow it to keep growing, providing more harvests later in the year.

Pairs with: Apple, strawberry, rhubarb, hawthorn flowers, elderflower, primrose, rosemary, maple and birch syrups, cream, wine, beer, rum, vodka, grappa and schnapps.

Locations: Dappled shade, often in woodland. Sweet woodruff is easy to grow in gardens.

Caution: As delicious as coumarin is, it comes with a warning: if you are drying sweet woodruff, make sure you dry it thoroughly, harvest it on a dry day, and keep it in a dry place in an airtight container. Sweet woodruff should be consumed in moderation and avoided if pregnant or on blood thinners.

How to drink: sweet woodruff

Fresh sweet woodruff imparts a delicate flavour to drinks but to get the most flavour from the plant, dry it in a low oven or dehydrator to release its flavours. Use sparingly; it has a surprisingly strong flavour.

 Wine: Sweet woodruff is used to flavour wines, making a celebratory springtime drink called maiwein in Germanic countries.

 Tea: Sweet woodruff tea has a long herbal tradition, used for its antispasmodic, anti-inflammatory and diuretic properties. Consumed in moderation, it is delicious paired with rosemary, birch leaves and a splash of maple syrup.

 Liqueurs: Sweet woodruff adds a delicious flavour to liqueurs, from neutral alcohol schnapps, to molasses-flavoured rum and even brandy. In Alsace, sweet woodruff is dried and soaked in sweetened brandy for up to 4 weeks, making a drink known as waldmeister.

 Bitters/tinctures: Covering the dried plant in a high-proof neutral spirit will make a vanilla-flavoured tincture, perfect for dropping into spiced warming cocktails.

 Cordials/syrups: Infusing the leaves and flowers in a sugar syrup makes a delicious addition to drinks. In Germany, the syrup is added to traditional Berliner weisse beers. Add a few stems of dried sweet woodruff or a drizzle of syrup to jugs of lemonade, making the perfect springtime soft drink.

May wine (maiwein)

May wine is a traditional German drink enjoyed on May Day (and beyond). This recipe uses dried leaves, but you can also use the fresh stems to infuse your drink, giving a slightly more herbal, fresh flavour. If you do, leave to infuse overnight.

_____

MAKES 1.5 LITRES (2³/₄ PINTS)
1 bottle of light white wine (a Riesling would
   be ideal)
7 dried sweet woodruff stems, plus extra
   to decorate
150g (5oz) strawberries
1 bottle of sparkling wine

Open the bottle of white wine and push the sweet woodruff into the bottle. Reseal and leave to infuse for 2 hours.

Chop the strawberries into a jug, add the sparkling wine and pour over the infused wine, straining out the herbs. Serve immediately with sprigs of woodruff to decorate.

Sweet woodruff & rosemary cream liqueur

Sweet woodruff is delicious when paired with woody rosemary in a cream-based drink. Sip it by itself or use to sweeten rather indulgent iced coffees.

_____

MAKES 1.1 LITRES (1 PINT 18FL OZ)
10 dried sweet woodruff stems
A few rosemary leaves
200ml (7fl oz) vodka
350ml (12fl oz) double cream
397g (14 oz) can condensed milk
250ml (9fl oz) hazelnut or acorn liqueur

Put the sweet woodruff and rosemary in a large jar, cover with the vodka and leave to infuse for 2 hours before straining. Pour the cream, condensed milk, liqueur and infused vodka into a bowl and whisk together until fully combined. Decant into sterilized bottles and store in the fridge for up to 4 weeks.

Summer

This is the season of abundant flowers and aromatic herbs. From early in the morning, through the day and into the night, the countryside becomes heavy with changing scents: oils released from drying hay, nectar-rich honeysuckle, the early-morning pollen of elderflowers and oil-plumped roses suspended in the warm air. It's not just flowers that are full of intoxicating scent; herbs like yarrow, mint, thyme and mugwort contain aromatic oils and incredible flavours. Take a walk in the height of summer and your olfactory senses will inhale a botanical feast that might just provide inspiration for a very seasonal vermouth or two.

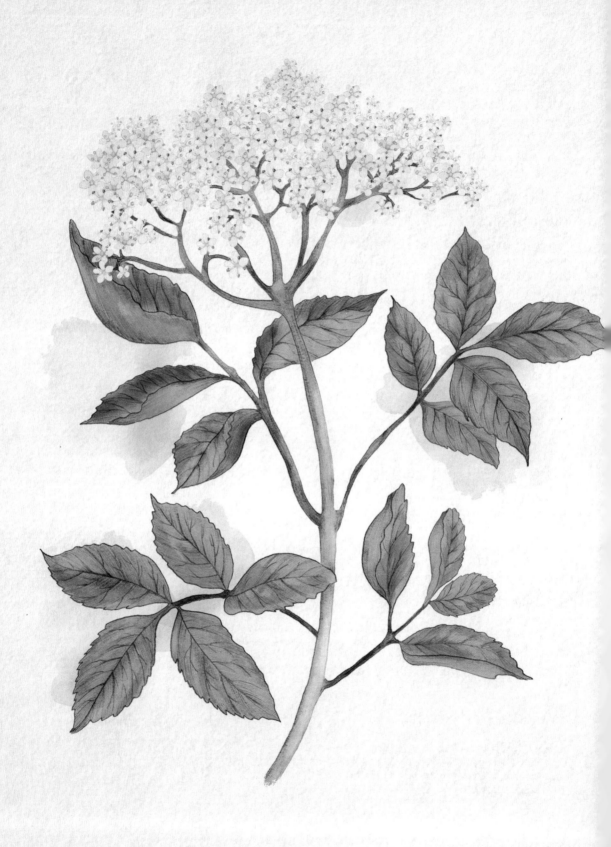

Elder (flower)
Sambucus spp.

Elder can grow as a small tree or, if pruned, as a shrub. The older branches are fissured (grooved) and grey, sending out new green growth each year that bears the fragrant flowers in summer and, ultimately, fruit. Elder leaves are divided into smaller leaflets and each leaf stem has five to seven lance-shaped leaflets arranged in pairs with one leaflet at the top.

The prized flowers open in umbels, with individual flowers spreading out on stalks from a central stem. When first open, they are pale cream, covered in yellow pollen and full of flavour – they need to be preserved quickly to keep it. Infusing the flowers isn't the only way to preserve them. You can also dry them for use later in the year to make out-of-season syrups, wines and immune-boosting teas. They burn easily, so dry in a dehydrator on a low setting, around 45°C (113°F), or in an airing cupboard. The flowers of pink-flowering elderflower (*Sambucus nigra* f. *porphyrophylla*), known as pink lace, taste like a combination of strawberry and elderflower. They make beautiful drinks such as liqueurs and cordials.

Edible parts: Flowers in early summer and berries in the autumn (see page 149).

Harvesting: Pick the flowers as they open in late spring to early summer, gathering them on a dry morning after the dew has dried off. Only collect flowers with pollen still on them and place on a tray to allow insects to crawl away. (Dipping them in water for a second will also work.) Pull the flowers away from as much of the stalk as possible and use them as quickly as you can.

Pairs with: Cucumber, rhubarb, gooseberry, strawberry, melon, ginger, lemon verbena, mint, lemon balm, wine, ginger beer and apple juice.

Locations: Elder grows in most temperate and subtropical areas of the world.

Caution: Take care to correctly identify. A number of toxic umbel-shaped flowers open at the same time and they often grow near each other. The flowers and berries are the only edible parts and elderberries need cooking before use (see page 149).

How to drink: elderflower

Elderflowers contain both sweet and savoury flavours: their sweet notes are fruity and floral, but rub a flower and you'll also smell a smoky, thyme scent that adds rounded flavours to sweet drinks.

Wine: Elderflower wine is one of the most lovely floral wines, made with fresh or dried elderflowers.

Liqueurs: To make elderflower liqueur, infuse the flowers (without stalks) by packing in a jar and covering with a neutral spirit. Leaving for even just an hour will pull out the best of the elderflower flavour. Strain and sweeten with a sugar syrup or light honey and keep on your cocktail shelf.

Cordials/syrups: Elderflower cordial is one of the most reached-for drinks of the summer. It freezes well in containers to be used later in the year when it might be needed to soothe symptoms of winter viruses.

Tea: Using fresh or dried flowers, elderflower tea can be made as an overnight cold infusion or with hot water, steeped for 10 minutes. It calms nerves, reduces anxiety and is also used to reduce inflammation and symptoms of colds, hay fever and flu. Blend with mint and lemon balm for a soothing, cooling summer drink.

Fermented drinks: Full of natural yeasts, elderflowers are perfect for making wild sodas, kvass and champagne. To make elderflower champagne, follow the recipe on page 73 and omit the rose petals. The flowers also make a lovely secondary flavouring in kombucha, kefir and ginger beer.

Vinegars: Infusing elderflowers and sugar or honey in apple cider vinegar makes a delicious cooling base for shrubs. Drink diluted like cordial or splash into cocktails for acidity. Elderflower vinegar can also be used as a salad dressing, which you can drink off the plate at the end!

Salts/sugars: Blitz an equal amount of dried flowers and salt together with a pinch of dried lemon zest and sprinkle into drinks or use as a salt rim on a Martini glass.

Instant elderflower limoncello

Elderflower's floral flavours almost instantly infuse into liqueurs. Longer soaks start to draw out the tannic, bitter compounds which, while being very good for you, make your drink less palatable. Once you taste elderflower-soaked vodka after an hour of infusing, you'll be a convert.

MAKES 500ML (18FL OZ)
75g (2¹/₂oz) elderflowers
250ml (9fl oz) vodka
100ml (3¹/₂fl oz) lemon juice
100ml (3¹/₂fl oz) water
100g (3¹/₂oz) caster sugar

Collect enough pollen-laden, freshly opened elderflowers to fill a 500ml (18fl oz) jar. To get the best flavour, remove them from the stalks and place them in the jar as you're collecting. Pour over the vodka and press a disc of baking paper into the top to make sure the flowers are submerged. Place the jar in direct sunlight, ideally outside, and infuse for at least 20 minutes, but not more than an hour.

Meanwhile, make a lemon syrup by mixing together the lemon juice, water and sugar, stirring until the sugar has dissolved. Strain the elderflower vodka and the lemon syrup through a sieve lined with fine muslin into a sterilized bottle. Serve immediately over lots of ice, with an obligatory elderflower decoration, or store for up to 6 months at room temperature (although it is best drunk within a month). You may want to boost the elderflower flavour if it has been stored by adding a drizzle of elderflower cordial when serving.

Elderflower cordial

Homemade elderflower cordial is a million miles better than anything you can buy in the shops. Although it should keep until the following harvest (if poured hot into sterilized bottles and pasteurized, see page 235), freezing the cordial in plastic containers until needed keeps the flavour when it is at its peak.

MAKES 2 LITRES (3¹/₂ PINTS)
1.5 litres (2³/₄ pints) water
1kg (2lb 4oz) sugar
Flowers from 25 elderflower heads,
    pulled from the stems
200ml (7fl oz) fresh lemon juice
Zest of 2 lemons

Heat the water in a saucepan, pour in the sugar and bring to a simmer, stirring until it has fully dissolved. Take the pan off the heat and allow to cool until the syrup is warm. Stir in the elderflowers, zest and half of the lemon juice. Cover and leave the flowers to infuse into the syrup overnight.

The next day, taste the cordial and add more of the lemon juice if necessary. Strain through a sieve lined with a double layer of muslin into a clean pan. Place the pan over a low heat until it is hot to the touch – you don't want the syrup to boil – and maintain this temperature for at least 10 minutes. If you have a food probe, it should be at least 60°C (140°F). Pour the cordial into freshly sterilized bottles when it is still hot. Seal the bottles and turn them upside down to form a sterile seal.

If you are freezing the cordial, make sure to use freezer-safe containers and leave space for at least 10 per cent expansion as the cordial freezes.

Rose (petal)
Rosa spp.

From the demure wild roses of early summer to the flamboyant garden varieties, all roses are edible – with as wide a selection of flavours as there are colours and flower shapes. The huge range we have today exists because we have cultivated them for thousands of years, for medicine, food, perfume and, of course, to drink. Rose petals are rich in minerals, vitamins and antioxidants, and have soothing properties. In Ayurvedic medicine, rose petals are often infused into milk drinks to soothe, cool and calm.

Cultivated, blousy roses are easy to identify in gardens; their wild cousins hidden among hedgerows are easier to miss. Often with small, simple flowerheads in shades of white and pink, wild roses usually only flower for a couple of weeks but luckily they often coincide with elderflower season – the flavour of wild roses and elderflowers together is one of the treats of summer. Rose flavour can dominate so use sparingly, leaving plenty of flowers to pollinate and turn into fruity rosehips (but that's for another season, see page 195).

Edible parts: The flower petals, leaves and rosehips (see page 192).

Harvesting: Collect roses on dry mornings when the petals are still plump and before the essential oils evaporate. Leave them on a shallow tray for an hour or so to allow any bugs to escape. The base of the petals where they join the flower head can be quite bitter. Snip them away from the flower heads leaving the bottom of the petals behind.

Pairs with: Elderflower, citrus, cardamom, saffron, milk, vanilla, strawberry, apple, plum, damson, chocolate, dandelion root, burdock root, fennel and cucumber.

Locations: Gardens, hedgerows and scrubland.

Caution: Roses are often treated with toxic chemicals – only harvest from plants that haven't been sprayed and never eat roses that have come from a florist.

How to drink: rose petal

All roses have their own unique flavours – some are sweet, some musky and others fruity. If you grow a variety of roses, use them in a blend to give you a delicious rounded flavour.

 Wine: Rose petal wine is often made with a grape juice base, the perfect foil for the heady perfume. Recent research has suggested that adding rose petals to grape wines helps increase their polyphenol and antioxidant content.

 Warming/milky drinks: Rose petals have a long history of being added to milk and yogurt drinks: from falooda made with vermicelli noodles and basil seeds, sahlab thickened with orchid roots, to lassi flavoured with cardamom and fruits.

 Liqueurs: Rose petals make great-tasting liqueurs. Either plunge them into a neutral grain alcohol for a couple of hours before adding sweetness, or stir spent petals from syrup making into the alcohol.

 Fermented drinks: Add rose petals to the second stage of making kombucha and water kefir. If you want to add fruit flavours along with the rose petals, try rhubarb, strawberries or cherries.

 Cordials/syrups: Infuse rose petals in a warm, heavy syrup made with sugar, water, orange juice and lemon juice overnight to create a lovely flavouring to add to milky drinks, sparkling wines and cocktails.

 Vinegars: Diluted with water as a shrub or splashed in a cocktail such as a Gin Fizz, sweet rose petal vinegars are among the most cooling drinks of the summer.

 Tea: Add fresh or dried petals and leaves to tea blends including herbal and black teas. Lay them in a single layer on a tray and dehydrate on a low setting for 12 hours, until the petals have shrunk and become crumbly. Store immediately in an airtight jar away from direct sunlight.

 Bitters/tinctures: Blend whole rose petals (including the bitter parts, see page 71) with other summer flavours like yarrow, burdock leaf, mugwort and orange peel to make a bottle of beautifully floral cocktail bitters.

Rose petal & elderflower champagne

If you head out at dawn on a summer morning, you might discover it is heavy with the scent of elderflowers and roses. If you do, you'll be in no doubt that rose petals and elderflowers make the most beautiful midsummer flavour combination.

_____

MAKES ABOUT 6.5 LITRES (11^1/$_2$ PINTS)
5 large or 10 small elderflower heads
2 litres (3^1/$_2$ pints) hot water
700g (1lb 9oz) sugar
2 tablespoons white wine vinegar
Juice and pared zest of 4 lemons
15g (^{1}/$_2$oz) rose petals
Pinch of wine yeast, if needed

Pull the elderflowers from the stems, discarding as much stalk as possible. Pour the water and sugar into a sterilized 6 litre (10^1/$_2$ pint) container, stirring to dissolve the sugar, then top up with 3.5 litres (6^1/$_4$ pints) of cold water. Stir in the vinegar, lemon juice and zest and gently stir through the flowers and petals. Cover with a fine cloth and place in a cool place for 4 days, stirring daily with a sterilized spoon to check the flowers are submerged.

By the fourth day you should start to see bubbles on the surface; if you don't, add a pinch of wine yeast to start fermentation. Strain the liquid through a sieve lined with a double layer of muslin into sterilized plastic bottles (in case you have an explosion). Seal the lids and store the bottles in a cool place, regularly checking for pressure build-up – plastic bottles will become hard to press. Release any gases that build up to prevent the champagne from exploding. It should be ready to drink after 2 weeks, then store in the fridge for up to a month.

Rose petal & cardamom yogurt drink

Roses are used to soothe and calm in Ayurvedic medicine, but they are also added to nourishing ice-cold yoghurt drinks to provide delicious respite from hot summer days.

_____

SERVES 2
50g (2oz) rose petals (freshly picked or frozen)
200ml (7fl oz) milk
^{1}/$_4$ teaspoon ground cardamom
2 teaspoons sugar (or other sweetener)
200ml (7fl oz) strained natural yogurt
   (or milk kefir)
Ice cubes

Place the rose petals into a blender with the milk and blend until the petals have broken up (dark petals will turn the mixture pink). Add the cardamom, sugar and yogurt and blend again for a few seconds.

Half fill a glass with ice cubes and pour over the rose yogurt mixture; drink immediately.

Honeysuckle
Lonicera spp.

Honeysuckle fills the summer evening air with perfume and pollinators, along with the equally beautiful hawk-moths that flock to its fragrant blooms. The most commonly found species of honeysuckle – *Lonicera periclymenum* (also known as woodbine) – and Japanese honeysuckle (*L. japonica*) both flower prolifically. The cream-flowered Japanese honeysuckle has smaller flowers than its hedgerow counterparts but what it lacks in size, it makes up for in volume – so rampant is it that in America, Japanese honeysuckle is high on the invasive species list.

New hairless stems grow from old woody vines each year, with green or purple hues. They are lined with pairs of opposing oval leaves and flowers in groups from what look like bobbly nodules. Unopened honeysuckle flowers look like miniature shoehorns, which burst open at the tips, the petals curling back as they mature to expose long thin stamens covered in pollen. The benefits for pollinators are clear, but they're also important for people. With antiviral, anti-inflammatory and throat-soothing properties, a basket of honeysuckle can be turned into drinks that make you feel better.

Edible parts: Flowers; certain species are bred for edible berries, buy from a specialist.

Harvesting: Pick honeysuckle with all the other creatures that need it in mind, only gathering what's in reach and leaving behind most of what you could collect.

Pairs with: Lilac, blackcurrant leaves, pine, strawberry, peach, nectarine, apricot, damson, plum, melon, vanilla, tarragon, mint, lemon balm, lemon verbena, black tea, coffee, gin, rum, whisky and beer.

Locations: Global temperate regions.

Caution: There are a wide range of cultivars of honeysuckle, some of which are toxic, so only gather from species known to be edible. The leaves and berries of most species of honeysuckle are not edible, so only gather the flowers.

How to drink: honeysuckle

Each honeysuckle flower contains a tiny drop of sweet nectar but the petals are a more substantial prize, tasting perfumed and floral with a hint of bitterness. The little green balls at the ends are bitter, so pull them away before using.

Wine: Honeysuckle makes one of the finest floral wines. Make with tea as your tannic addition and with orange for acidic balance.

Beer: Adding honeysuckle to citrusy beers with the hops will give a wisp of perfume that balances the bitter citrus flavours. Or pour a dash of honeysuckle syrup into an ice-cold lager to make a shandy with style.

Liqueurs: Honeysuckle makes a wonderful liqueur on its own in rum or clear spirits, but add a twist of orange peel, peaches or strawberries to make a sweet version. It also pairs well with autumnal fruits – try adding a handful to a jar of damsons soaking in gin. Also try the flowers in vermouth, amaro, orange liqueur and Campari.

Cordials/syrups: Honeysuckle syrup is indispensable as a flavouring for food and drink, as well as an ambrosial linctus for sore throats and coughs.

Tea: Infuse the flowers into hot or cold teas. If you want a hot tea, leave the kettle to cool for a few minutes before pouring the water over the flowers. The dried flowers can be added to dried teas – try with black tea, pine needles or blackcurrant leaves.

Fermented drinks: Ferment into wild champagnes, wild sodas, kefir, kvass and kombucha.

Bitters/tinctures: Pair honeysuckle with bitter roots such as dandelion or artichoke; or burdock leaf, orange peel and yarrow or mugwort to make a bitter tincture to add summer floral notes to cocktails.

Salts/sugars: Fresh flowers are best: pound them with a pestle and mortar until broken down, add sugar or salt and use while still damp, or leave on a flat plate to dry and use later in the year. Perfect for finishing drinks.

Honeysuckle kombucha

This tannic ferment delivers a refreshing drink that you can still make with dried flowers when honeysuckle isn't in season. It can be paired with strawberries, peaches, pineapple weed, tarragon, blackcurrant leaves or mint – simply add them with the honeysuckle flowers.

MAKES 2 LITRES (3¹/₂ PINTS)
1 litre (1³/₄ pints) boiling unchlorinated water
4 tablespoons tea leaves
15g (¹/₂oz) sugar, plus extra for bottling
1 kombucha SCOBY, plus 500ml (18fl oz) retained
   liquid from the previous first ferment
75g (2¹/₂oz) fresh honeysuckle flowers, or half
   the amount of dried flowers

Pour the just-boiled water over the tea, stir and leave to infuse for 15 minutes before straining. Discard the leaves and pour the tea into a sterilized 2 litre (3¹/₂ pint) container, add the sugar and stir until the sugar has dissolved. Top up with another 500ml (18fl oz) cold water, leaving space to add the SCOBY and kombucha liquid from the last time you used it. If you don't have any retained liquid, add more water. Cover the container with a clean cloth and leave to ferment for at least 5 days.

After the fifth day, taste the kombucha each day: once it has turned acidic, remove the SCOBY along with a cupful of the kombucha and place them both in a clean jar for another batch.

Pour the kombucha into a wide-necked bottle, add the honeysuckle flowers and another teaspoon of sugar and cover again for a few days before drinking, loosening the lid from time to time to release any excess pressure. Store in the fridge for up 2 weeks, during which time it will become more sour, and remember to keep loosening the lid.

Honeysuckle & poached white peach liqueur

White peaches and honeysuckle are beautiful together in drinks and desserts and, as luck would have it, this recipe gives you the best of both. You can easily swap the vodka for rum or tequila in this recipe if they're your spirit of choice.

MAKES 500ML (18FL OZ)
35g (1¹/₄oz) fresh honeysuckle flowers
300ml (¹/₂ pint) vodka
600ml (1 pint) water
200g (7oz) sugar
6 white peaches

Place half the honeysuckle flowers in a jar and cover with the vodka. Leave to infuse while you poach the peaches, but for no more than 2 hours.

Place the water and sugar in a saucepan and bring to a simmer, stirring, until the sugar has dissolved. Place the peaches in the syrup, cover and poach gently for 10 minutes. Turn off the heat, add the remaining honeysuckle flowers and leave the fruit and flowers to infuse in the syrup for 30 minutes.

Strain the syrup (you can serve the honeysuckle-infused peaches for dessert). Pour 200ml (7fl oz) of the syrup into a sterilized bottle with the strained vodka. Shake to mix the vodka and syrup together. This is best drunk immediately but will store out of sunlight for up to 6 months. Serve over ice or lengthen with cream soda.

Mahonia
Mahonia spp.

One of the common names you might know mahonia by is 'Oregon grape'. And if you've ever come across a mahonia dripping with ripe fruit, you'll know why: clusters of oval purple fruits with a white dusting hang from flower stems like grapes. The taste of the summer-ripening fruit is as sharp as the spines on the leaves. Crammed full of vitamin C, it's one of the most intensely sour flavours you can pluck from the wild, one which transforms into the most vibrant of purple colours and vibrant of flavoured drinks.

During the winter, mahonias are covered with yellow flowers that smell sweet and lemony, and taste the same. Wild mahonias are so prolific in the woods of Oregon that it's the state flower and they are often planted in towns as a living security fence – it's a brave (or foolish) soul who pushes through a mahonia hedge. A bitter chemical concentrated in the roots and wood called berberine is extracted into tinctures by herbalists who use it medicinally for a wide range of ailments.

Edible parts: Flowers, berries and roots (used sparingly).

Harvesting: The berries ripen over a couple of weeks in summer. Pick every few days, as they soften. Freezing before use brings out a sweeter flavour. Use or dry the flowers as you gather them in autumn and winter.

Pairs with: Fruit with lemon, apple, grape, sweet blueberry, kiwi, plum, blackberry, mint, lemon balm, lemon grass, vanilla, elderflower, cardamom and juniper. Flowers with lemon, apple, quince, pear and evergreen firs such as spruces and pines.

Locations: In their native environment, mahonias grow in dappled shaded woodland; otherwise found in gardens and urban planting schemes.

Caution: Due to the berberine content, avoid when pregnant or breastfeeding. Do not give to young children or consume if you have a liver condition.

How to drink: mahonia

The flowers and berries have contrasting flavours – the flowers are light, with a hint of sherbet, while the berries are bitterly sour.

Wine: Mahonia berries make a deeply flavoured fruit wine, while the flowers make a light floral wine.

Liqueurs: Treat mahonia berries like sloes to make mahonia gin. The flowers are lovely infused into light, floral gins.

Cocktails: Freeze mahonia berries to use as sour bursts of flavour in cocktails, from Daiquiris to Mojitos. A handful of berries will burst open to colour and flavour all sorts of drinks.

Cordials/syrups: Both the flowers and berries can be infused into floral and incredibly fruity syrups and cordials. Pair both fruit and flowers with lemons to add acidity to the flowers and fruitiness to the astringent berries.

Tea: The yellow roots of mahonia are used as a medicinal tea to treat a wide range of ailments. They are sometimes drunk blended with black tea for a mellow flavour.

Fermented drinks: Mahonia flowers ferment into delicious wild sodas and, if left for a couple of weeks, a floral champagne-style lightly alcoholic drink to enjoy in the early winter when little else is in bloom.

Bitters/tinctures: Mahonia roots are bitter and often sold as extracts for herbal treatments. A drop of mahonia bitters is delicious in a cocktail.

Mahonia flower bee's knees

Mahonia flowers provide important food for bees during the colder months. If you have an abundance of blooms, pluck a few to make this lemon and honey cocktail. The leftover mahonia flower-infused syrup from can be added to a warming lemon and honey drink.

SERVES 2
150ml (5fl oz) honey
150ml (5fl oz) water
4 mahonia flower stems, plus extra to decorate
120ml (4fl oz) light gin
40ml (1½fl oz) lemon juice
Ice cubes

To make the syrup, put the honey and water in a pan and heat until the honey has become runny. Stir to combine and take off the heat. Stir in the flowers plucked from three of the mahonia stems, cover and leave overnight to infuse. The next day, strain the syrup into a sterilized bottle (this will keep for up to 1 month in the fridge).

To make the Bee's Knees cocktail, place the gin, lemon juice and 40ml (1½fl oz) of the infused honey syrup into a cocktail shaker with the remaining flower stem and some ice (adding a dash of mahonia root extract as bitters if you have any). Shake and strain into two chilled cocktail glasses, then decorate with a few mahonia flowers.

Mahonia berry syrup

Mahonia berry syrup is unapologetically intense – it'll add astringent, bitter and sour flavours to drinks as well as turning them purply-pink. Add a drizzle of the syrup to Mojitos, sparkling wine or grape juice with club soda to make a non-alcoholic Bellini.

MAKES 250ML (9FL OZ)
200g (7oz) ripe mahonia berries
250ml (9fl oz) water
50ml (2fl oz) lemon juice
About 250g (9oz) sugar

Pull the berries from the stems, wash them, then freeze and thaw before use to sweeten them.

Place the berries and water in a saucepan on a gentle heat. Once the water boils, remove from the heat and use a fork to break apart the berries. Add the lemon juice and leave to steep for 2 hours.

Strain the liquid into a measuring jug and note the amount before pouring back into the saucepan with an equal amount of sugar to juice – for example, 250g (9oz) of sugar to 250ml (9fl oz) of juice. Bring to a gentle simmer, stirring to dissolve the sugar, then pour into a sterilized bottle. Seal and cool before storing in the fridge for up to 3 weeks.

Meadowsweet
Filipendula ulmaria

Meadowsweet is one of the many useful edible plants in the rose family (Rosaceae), which also includes plums, apples and cherries. Meadowsweet's flowers have the same almond flavouring, which sweetens with hints of hay when they're dried. Although you'll find meadowsweet in meadows, it's a lover of wet soil, thriving where its roots can be damp in boggy fields, pond edges and ditches. Less romantically, it's also called 'Queen of the Ditch'.

Look close up at the tiny, five-petalled flowers and you'll see they are filled with up to twenty long sepals. The flowers grow in frothy clusters perched on thin, red stems which rise from the wet ground. You can harvest a more medicinal flavour from the pairs of oval serrated leaves growing along the red leaf stems, alternating between large and tiny sets of leaves. Give them a rub and you'll release their unique scent – a cross between Germolene and saffron. These leaves that are rich in salicylic acid and have been used for thousands of years as an anti-inflammatory painkiller. They were the first plants used to make aspirin.

Edible parts: Flowers, stems and leaves.

Harvesting: Only take small amounts of this important food source for pollinators. Pick on dry days and avoid gathering any that has a white mildew covering. The leaves can be harvested in spring to autumn, the flowers in mid to late summer, with the largest harvest in midsummer.

Pairs with: Rosebay willow herb, cherry, honeysuckle, rose, apple, strawberry, vanilla, rhubarb, orange, lemon, ginger and turmeric.

Locations: Damp meadows, wetlands, ditches, verges and lanes.

Caution: Avoid using meadowsweet if you are allergic to aspirin or pregnant. Certain mould spores can convert the coumarin into a strong blood thinner, so make sure to never harvest if mildewy, and discard any dried material that has become damp.

How to drink: meadowsweet

If using fresh, store meadowsweet in the fridge in an airtight container for a few days. Or, dry the flowers and leaves as soon as you harvest them, on the lowest setting of a dehydrator, placed on a piece of baking paper to capture all of the pollen and petals. Store in an airtight jar for up to a year.

 Beer: Meadowsweet has a long tradition of being used in herbal beers and mead; use sparingly so as not to overpower the other herbs and flavours in the drinks.

 Liqueurs: Infuse into everything from gin- and vodka-based liqueurs to darker spirits such as rum and whisky. Use the flowers rather than leaves and stems and only soak them in your chosen spirit for a couple of hours at the most before straining. Start by using 2 teaspoons of fresh or 1 teaspoon of dried flowers per 500ml (18fl oz) of spirit. Add a fresh batch of flowers if needed to the strained spirit to strengthen the herb's flavour after tasting.

 Cordials/syrups: Meadowsweet cordial tastes honeyed with hints of vanilla and almond. Using only the flowers will give the best flavour. Dried flowers add a hint of hay.

 Tea: Meadowsweet leaf tea is often drunk for aches and pains. Should you want to drink it for its herbal benefits, try it paired with an equally potent anti-inflammatory such as nettle. In Russia, it is paired with rosebay willow herb, two beautiful summer plants in flower at the same time.

 Fermented drinks: Add a teaspoon of meadowsweet flowers to the second fermentation of kombuchas and kvass drinks. Meadowsweet makes a delicious low-alcohol champagne (use it in place of rose and elderflower in the recipe on page 73).

 Bitters/tinctures: Meadowsweet is so strong that you only need a single drop of the extract to add an almond flavour to drinks. Place dried flowers into a jar, cover with vodka and leave to soak for a week.

Midsummer cocktail

If you ever head out to forage on a warm midsummer night, you will find your basket full of flowers, herbs and fruits. This drink is less of a recipe and more of a call to turn those finds into a delicious toast to the height of summer. If you can't find all the ingredients, don't panic – this is a celebration of your midsummer, not mine. Just use what you can find.

───────

SERVES 4

1 stem of meadowsweet flowers, plus extra
   to decorate
1 handful of clover flowers
1 handful of honeysuckle flowers
2 stems of pineapple weed flowers
1 handful of linden flowers
2 stems of yarrow flowers
1 handful of wild strawberries, or 5 strawberries,
   cut into small pieces
4 cherries
2 tablespoons elderflower cordial (see page 69)
200ml (7fl oz) vodka
Ice cubes
750ml (1 pint 7fl oz) sparkling water
4 pieces of mugwort or burdock leaf, to serve

Place the flowers, herbs and fruit in a jug and use a muddling stick or bottom of a rolling pin to smash them, to release their flavours. Pour over the elderflower cordial and vodka. Leave to infuse for 15 minutes before straining.

   Fill four glasses with ice, add the infused elderflower and vodka and top up with ice-cold sparkling water. Add a piece of mugwort or burdock leaf to each drink for people to remove when their drinks are bitter enough for their taste. Decorate with a sprinkle of meadowsweet flowers.

Meadowsweet & autumn fruit immuni-tea

While the main display of meadowsweet comes in the middle of summer, the flowers keep blooming until the ripe fruits of autumn are hanging heavy in the hedgerows. Paired with immune-boosting elderberries and blackberries, nutritious nettles and sweetly antioxidant vanilla, meadowsweet makes a warming and sweet tea that is as delicious soaked in hot apple juice with brandy or rum as a toddy as it is with just-boiled water. Make sure that your fruit is thoroughly dried so that you don't add moisture to the meadowsweet. You can make this tea with fresh ingredients, following the same proportions.

───────

FILLS A 250ML (9FL OZ) JAR

2 tablespoons dried meadowsweet flowers
2 tablespoons dried nettle leaves, finely crumbled
$1/2$ dried vanilla pod, crumbled
4 tablespoons dried elderberries
8 tablespoons dried blackberries, broken apart

Place all the ingredients into a large bowl and stir so that the flowers and leaves are combined with the berries. Spoon into an airtight jar and store out of direct sunlight.

   Make the tea by soaking 1 heaped teaspoon per person in just-boiled water for 10 minutes before straining.

Clover
Trifolium pratense, T. repens

Clover has oval-shaped, sometimes rounded and other times more pointed leaves with a pale chevron arrow pointing through each leaf. The leaves are usually (but as four-leafed clover hunters will attest, not always) in sets of three. During the summer, they grow ball-like clusters of tiny tubular flowers which are full of nectar, attracting honey bees and other pollinators. Part of the vast pea, or legume, family, there are over 300 different clovers and many are edible but, as with lots of plants, some are not.

Fortunately the two most common clovers spanning the globe are edible. Red clover (*Trifolium pratense*) and its shorter sibling white clover (*Trifolium repens*) are both easy to find. They have a sweet taste with a hint of pea when fresh but, when dried, they taste more like a cross between vanilla and the scent of drying hay. If you've ever stood near a meadow as the freshly cut sward is drying, you'll know this heady scent, which is due to the chemical coumarin being released. Clover is medicinal and herbalists gather the flowers to use for their blood-purifying properties, for bone health and to help balance oestrogen levels.

Edible parts: Flowers and leaves.

Harvesting: Pick clover on warm, dry days and process the same day. Harvest the flowers when they are just opening and not browned as this will affect the flavour.

Pairs with: Fresh flowers: with strawberry, melon, cucumber, lemon and gin. Dried flowers: with thyme, oregano, yarrow, meadowsweet, dairy, rum and brandy.

Locations: Clover grows in most grasslands – from lawns to pastures.

Caution: If exposed to damp, coumarin in clover can develop blood-thinning properties. Make sure to harvest plants that do not have mildew and, if storing, dry it thoroughly as soon as you have harvested it. Clover is best avoided by people on blood thinners, those who are pregnant or have certain hormone-related cancers.

How to drink: clover

Fresh clover flowers are in season through the summer. To dry them for use later in the year, harvest on a dry day, place the flowers on a low setting in a dehydrator and dry until they are crumbly. Seal the flowers in an airtight container and store in a dry place away from direct sun.

Wine: Red clover is traditionally made into a floral wine; add orange and lemon for acidity and flavour.

Liqueurs: Dry clover flowers infused into neutral spirits give a gentle honeyed flavour, much like the famous bison grass vodkas. The Islay-based Botanist gin includes foraged white and red clover flowers among the botanicals used to add a sweetness to the spirit.

Cordials/syrups: Both fresh and dried clover flowers can be used to make clover syrup. Dried clover syrup tastes like the scent of hay. Both syrups are best made by making a tea infusion with the flowers before adding the sugar.

Tea: Red and white clover flowers are picked when they have just opened and are dried to make tea. Drink hot or cold with a spoonful of honey or slice of orange. Clover flowers pair beautifully with yarrow and lemon balm in teas.

Warming/milky drinks: Dried clover flowers ground to a powder make a lovely flavouring for cold and warm milky drinks.

Vinegars: Clover flowers are added to oxymels, made with a blend of vinegar, honey and herbs. This mixture is infused to extract flavour, nutrition and medicinal properties from plants. Cover a jar of flowers with equal parts vinegar and honey, then leave to infuse for 3–4 weeks before straining. Clover oxymel is lovely diluted into apple juice or added to cocktails.

Red clover lemonade

Red clover lemonade is made with a slowly infused tea that draws out the flavour and nutrients of the flower. Delicious, cooling and rich in minerals and vitamins, it's an ideal restorative drink for hot summer days.

MAKES 1 LITRE (1³/₄ PINTS)
75g (2¹/₂oz) freshly picked
   clover flowers
900ml (1 pint 11fl oz) boiling water
100g (3¹/₂oz) sugar
Juice of 4 lemons
Lemon balm or mint sprigs
Ice cube, to serves

Place the clover flowers in a colander and rinse under cold water to get rid of any dust. Put the flowers into a large jar and pour over the just-boiled water. Leave to cool before sealing and placing in the fridge overnight.

   The next day, strain the infused tea. Place the sugar in the jar with the strained clover tea and stir until the sugar has dissolved. Add the lemon juice and watch the drink turn pink as it reacts with the acid. Serve in tumblers with a few lemon balm or mint sprigs and some ice.

Haymaker cocktail

Harvesting hay comes in the heat of the summer and is a hot, tiring job. There's not much better to quench your thirst than a cold cider at the end of a harvest day – especially if that cider is turned into a Haymaker, with a generous pour of vodka and sweet clover syrup.

SERVES 2
250ml (9fl oz) water
150g (5oz) sugar
25g (1oz) dried clover flowers
60ml (2fl oz) vodka
500ml (18fl oz) chilled dry cider
Ice cubes, to serve

To make a clover syrup, place the water and sugar in a saucepan and heat gently, stirring, until the sugar dissolves and the liquid becomes clear. Take off the heat, stir in the flowers and leave overnight to infuse. Strain the syrup into a sterilized bottle and store in the fridge for up to a month.

   To make the Haymaker cocktail, fill two tall glasses with ice. Divide the vodka and 50ml (2fl oz) of the clover syrup between the glasses and stir until they are well blended. Pour over the cider, stir again and serve. Best enjoyed while leaning against a haystack.

Pineapple weed
Matricaria discoidea

Pineapple weed lacks the showy white petals of its siblings German and Roman chamomile (see page 115), looking like they've been cruelly pulled off, leaving behind green-yellow domes. This plant is likely to be found cropping up in the least hospitable stony ground, tracks, gateways and even popping up through cracks in urban streets – a skill that has earned the plant the names of 'street weed' and 'pavement weed'. Each of the petal-less flowerheads produces hundreds of seeds, spread about as people and animals move around, which is why you'll find it in so many places.

The seeds that germinate will start to grow the following spring, first forming basal rosettes of hairless feathered leaves which, by summer, produce flowering stems growing up to 30cm (12in) tall. Although the flowers don't look much, pineapple weed comes into its own when in bloom. Fresh pineapple weed is sweetly herbal, pineapple-y fruity and utterly scrumptious – proof you don't need to live in the best spots or be the best dressed to be desired.

Edible parts: Leaves, stems and flowers.

Harvesting: Pineapple weed has shallow roots and pulls up from the ground very easily. To avoid uprooting the plant, and to encourage more growth, use scissors to harvest the tender leaves and flowers in midsummer to early autumn.

Pairs with: Mint, nettle, clover, fennel, cucumber, meadowsweet, melon, apple, pineapple, mango, apricot, peach, cream, rum, gin, wine and strawberry.

Locations: Footpaths, gateways and compacted poor soil.

Caution: Pineapple weed is part of the Asteraceae (daisy) family. Take care not to confuse the young plant for groundsel (*Senecio vulgaris*) or ragwort (*Jacobaea vulgaris*). Do not use it if you are allergic to this family of plants.

How to drink: pineapple weed

Pineapple weed's fresh leaves and flowers are delightfully fruity with a slight astringency; drying intensifies the flavour of the flowers. To dry them, lay them on baking paper to capture the flowerheads if they crumble and dry in a gentle heat away from direct sun.

Tea: Pineapple weed, like chamomile, has soothing properties which promote calming and restful sleep. While you can make pineapple weed tea with fresh flowers, drying brings out a more intense flavour. Pineapple weed blends well with thyme, fennel and nettle seeds. For a soothing night-time brew, combine one part pineapple weed with equal parts linden flowers and lemon balm.

Champagne: Pineapple weed makes a delicious herbal champagne, especially if paired with elderflower.

Liqueurs: Soak pineapple weed in a neutral alcohol such as grappa or vodka for 24 hours to extract its sweet fruity flavour into the spirit. The sweet flavour means you can use less sweetener than in other liqueurs – try sweetening with a splash of apple juice.

Cordials/syrups: Dried and fresh pineapple weed make delicious syrups to add to cocktails and soft drinks.

Fermented drinks: Fresh and dried pineapple weed are lovely added to fermented drinks such as tepache, ginger beer and water kefir.

Vinegars: Infuse pineapple weed into a sweetened vinegar with honey to make an oxymel or shrub.

Salts/sugars: Fresh pineapple weed flowers or even tough stems can be ground up with salt and dried in a low oven to make a seasoning salt for cocktails.

Pineapple weed margarita

Some herbs need cajoling to provide their flavour, while others give it generously and easily – and not many more so than pineapple weed, which simply needs muddling and a quick infusion to impart its flavour. It's particularly tasty when paired with tequila in a Margarita.

————

SERVES 2
100ml (3½fl oz) tequila reposado
40ml (1½fl oz) triple sec
20g (¾oz) fresh pineapple weed flowerheads, plus extra to decorate
Pineapple weed flower salt (see opposite page)
50ml (2fl oz) lime juice
Ice cubes

Pour the tequila and triple sec into a cocktail shaker; add the fresh flowerheads and use a muddling stick to lightly mash the flowers into the liquid. Leave to infuse for 10 minutes.

Sprinkle a layer of pineapple weed flower salt on a plate. Dip the rims of two cocktail glasses in water, then dip in the pineapple weed salt to create a salt rim.

Add the lime juice and some ice to the cocktail shaker and shake for 30 seconds. Place an ice cube and a stem of pineapple weed in each of two glasses and strain over the drink, using a fine sieve to capture the broken flowers.

Pineapple weed milkshake

Pineapple weed's affinity with dairy turns a milkshake into a special treat that you could serve as a liquid dessert. Children and adults alike will thank you for the pairing. You can use almond milk and plant-based ice cream if you prefer.

————

SERVES 2
500ml (18fl oz) whole milk
2 teaspoons dried pineapple weed
200g (7oz) ice cream
Ice cubes
Fresh pineapple weed flowers, to decorate

Pour the milk into a saucepan and heat gently until it is warm to the touch. Remove from the heat, stir in the pineapple weed and leave to infuse for 15 minutes.

Strain the milk through a very fine sieve into a blender and leave to cool to room temperature, add the ice cream and blend until creamy. Pour into two chilled glasses over ice and garnish with fresh pineapple weed flowers. Drink immediately (or if you feel inclined, first stir in a measure of rum – no one will judge).

Wild strawberry
Fragaria spp.

From the start of spring, sometimes even in warm winters, wild strawberries start to flower with white, five-petalled flowers on straggly stems growing from clusters of classic strawberry-shaped leaves. They are often easier to locate when they're flowering than when they're in fruit because by the time their red berries form, they're often hidden among long grasses on the verges, woodland edges and fields they inhabit. If you do find wild strawberries in flower, come back in the middle of summer with a cupped hand or a little tub to gather a tiny, but rather mighty, crop of the fruit. Because what they lack in size, they make up in flavour.

There are two main species of wild strawberry: the alpine or woodland strawberry (*Fragaria vesca*) and the beach strawberry (*F. chiloensis*). Both are small and bear the fruits we used to eat before large, sweet, modern cultivated strawberries arrived on the scene. Wild strawberries come with a concentration of flavours – floral, almost rose-like, with an intense fruitiness. This is due both to strawberry's rose family membership and because they contain pinenes and terpenes, the same aroma compounds (called esters) that you find in plants like pine and bay, making even a tiny handful very worthwhile indeed.

Edible parts: Fruit, flowers and leaves.

Harvesting: Wild strawberries are at their most flavoursome when they are soft and starting to break down. Children in Scandinavia thread wild strawberries on stems of straw as they collect them. Harvest leaves and flowers in spring to autumn (or mild winters) and fruits in summer.

Pairs with: Pine, clover, pineapple weed, rose petals, tea, elderflower, yarrow, lemon, milk, vodka, aquavit, grappa and gin.

Locations: Grasslands, woodland edges and coastal grasslands.

Caution: Like cultivated strawberries, wild ones can cause a rash-like reaction. Avoid if you react to cultivated varieties. Don't use wilted leaves.

How to drink: wild strawberry

The leaves of wild strawberry have an astringent flavour with a hint of the fruit. The flowers are delicate and unless there is an abundance of flowers, it's better to leave them until they turn into fruit.

 Wine: Wild strawberries are beloved by winemakers for their fruity country-style wines. Add wild strawberries to vermouth (see page 113) for a dry, fruity flavour to balance the bitter ingredients.

 Liqueurs: Italian brand Fragolia macerate wild strawberries for four months to make their wild strawberry liqueur. Try macerating wild strawberries in a neutral spirit and sweeten with wild strawberry syrup to make a sweet, delicious liqueur, lovely served with a splash of cold yarrow tea to add an aromatic bitterness.

 Cordials/syrups: Tiny wild strawberries contain intense flavours that are best released into syrups by first macerating in sugar in a cheong-style technique (see opposite).

 Tea: Dried wild strawberry fruits are wonderful blended with black tea. The dried leaves are also drunk as a tonifying herbal tea, either by themselves or with other herbs including mint, cleavers and nettle.

 Warming/milky drinks: A few wild strawberries blended into full fat milk make a delicious drink. Try adding a few to the Pineapple weed milkshake on page 93 for a sweet, fruity, hay meadow flavour.

 Fermented drinks: Wild strawberries ferment into fruity, refreshing wild sodas. For every cup of wild strawberries, add ¼ cup of sugar and 3 cups of water. Place in a jar and ferment for a week, shaking and opening the lid each day. Strain out the berries, pour the liquid into sterilized bottles and allow the carbonation to develop for a day or so before drinking.

Wild strawberry cheong syrup

Cheongs are Korean fruit syrups, made by drawing the liquid from fruit into the sugar during a long slow maceration, rather than using heat. This method keeps the flavour of the fruits fresh and bright and strawberries are especially good used this way. Lemon is added to the fruit to add a balance of flavour and also to keep the syrup a vibrant colour. You can use cultivated strawberries for this recipe as well, or a blend of both.

_____

MAKES 150ML (5FL OZ)
100g (3^1/$_2$oz) soft wild strawberries, rinsed
^{1}/$_4$ unwaxed lemon, cut into small pieces
   (peel and flesh)
100g (3^1/$_2$oz) white sugar

Place the wild strawberries and lemon in a bowl. Sprinkle over half the sugar and stir until the fruit is fully coated. Spoon the mixture into a jar and pour over the remaining sugar, making sure the fruit is covered. Place in the fridge and leave to macerate for a few days until the sugar has dissolved. Stir in a splash of water if the sugar is not dissolving.

This syrup can be strained, or spooned straight into drinks with the pieces of fruit still in. Try spooning 2 teaspoons into a champagne flute and topping up with sparkling wine to make a wild strawberry royale.

Bay leaf, pine needle & wild strawberry tea

The shared compounds contained in bay, pine and wild strawberries come together to make a floral and fruity tea, also great as a cold infused drink – soak the leaves and berries overnight and drink straight or carbonated with gin. This recipe is for fresh tea, but you can dry the ingredients to make a tea to use through the year; just make sure that the fruit is completely dry before storing.

_____

SERVES 2
5 wild strawberries
10 wild strawberry leaves
^{1}/$_2$ bay leaf, ripped into small pieces
10 pine needles, rolled with a rolling pin to bruise

Place the ingredients in a small teapot, pour over just-boiled water and leave to brew for 5 minutes, before straining and drinking.

Mint
Mentha spp.

Mints are among the most commonly used herbs to flavour food and, of course, drinks. In fact, a botanically inclined bar may well have more than one kind of mint: there may be a bunch of mojito mint, or peppermint, chocolate mint or even banana mint, all giving their distinct flavour to a range of cocktails. Because of its ability to spread and hybridize, you might find a wide variety of mints in the wild, especially if you're harvesting near gardens where underground runners spread through flowerbeds and lawns.

Fortunately, there are a few traits that all mints share that will help you identify them. Firstly, rub the plant; only mints smell like mint. Look at the stem and leaves – while they can range in colour from dark green to purple, all mints have square stems with pairs of oval leaves growing opposite each other. The tiny flowers have four petals and are fused together like a trumpet; these flowers either grow in whorls around the stem, or in clusters at the tip of the plant. If you find one you particularly like the taste of, propagate a tiny cutting to start your own mint collection.

Edible parts: Leaves, stems and flowers.

Harvesting: Pick mints before they flower for the best flavour. If you keep cutting them back, you'll ensure a regular supply of leaves at their peak. Dry mints for teas to use during the winter.

Pairs with: Cucumber, elderflower, pineapple weed, linden, rose, cherry, wild strawberry, crab apple, birch, nettle, flowering currant, spruce, pine, blackcurrant, ground ivy, sorrel, fennel and blackberry.

Locations: Mint thrives in moist but well-drained soils, in full sun or partial shade. Mint spreads by runners and often forms large clumps.

Caution: Mint can interact with some medications.

How to drink: mint

While fresh mint has a vibrant taste, dried mint occupies a different place in the kitchen, developing a more mellow, woody flavour. When you harvest fresh mint, dry and store some for teas and drinks that need a more subtle taste.

Wine: Mint leaves brew into a light wine with a very subtle mint flavour, often drunk as a dessert wine.

Cocktails: Mints are among the most well-used herbs in cocktails, from Mint Juleps and Moscow Mules, to Gimlets and Mojitos. Most cocktails use spearmints, but corn mints (illustrated overleaf) provide a more fruity flavour.

Tea: The menthol in mint helps relax muscles and calm stress. Mint tea is drunk both for its calming properties and to sooth stomach complaints and ease symptoms of colds and flu. Moroccan mint tea (atay bi na'na) is made by steeping green tea leaves and fresh mint in just-boiled water, then sweetening it with 1 tablespoon of sugar per 250ml (9fl oz) of liquid.

Fermented drinks: Mints ferment into delicious drinks: from ginger beer to kombucha, milk and water kefir. You can add mint leaves to herbal meads (known as metheglins).

Bitters/tinctures: Infuse dried mint with lemon verbena, lime zest and cardamom in a high-proof neutral spirit for 2 weeks to make a bitters that adds a zesty, cooling flavour to drinks.

Juice: Try juicing mint with ginger, cucumber and apples, or turning your leaves into Verdita – a Mexican drink made by blending fresh mint with coriander, chilli and pineapple, traditionally served in shot glasses alongside tequila.

Crème de menthe

This iconic drink was first made in 1885 by French pharmacist Emile Giffard as a digestive health liqueur. It's now more commonly found in cocktail cabinets than medicine cupboards, often a bright green colour due to the addition of food colouring. This version is made by infusing mint into alcohol and sugar syrup, creating a clear but flavourful drink.

MAKES 600ML (1 PINT)
320ml (11fl oz) vodka
75g (2½oz) fresh spearmint or peppermint leaves
200g (7oz) white sugar
250ml (9fl oz) water

Pour the vodka into a jar and add one-third of the mint leaves, smacking each leaf before you submerge it into the vodka (this helps to release the oils). Make sure the mint is fully submerged by pressing a weight or a piece of baking paper on top.

Place the sugar and water in a saucepan on a medium heat and bring to a boil, stirring until the sugar dissolves. Remove the syrup from the heat and cool slightly before adding half the remaining mint leaves. Leave both the vodka and the syrup to infuse with the mint overnight.

The next day, strain the vodka and the sugar syrup and mix together. Pour into the jar, adding the final mint leaves; leave to infuse for 24 hours before straining through a fine sieve and transferring to a sterilized bottle. Crème de menthe is best stored in a cool place and drunk within a couple of months – it will keep indefinitely but its flavour will reduce over time.

Try using it to make a classic but simple drink – the Stinger. Mix 2 parts Cognac with 1 part crème de menthe and enjoy.

Frozen mint lemonade

Mint lemonade is an incredibly cooling drink consumed across the Middle East – the most delicious and vibrant slushy you'll find. Spearmint is the most widely used in this drink; if you don't have spearmint, choose a fruity, mild mint like apple mint. You can add other herbs to the blend – fennel, nettles and blackcurrant leaves all work really well in mint lemonade.

SERVES 4
400ml (14fl oz) lemon juice (about 8 lemons)
200g (7oz) sugar
25g (1oz) mint leaves (about 20 sprigs)
1 teaspoon orange blossom water (optional)
750ml (1 pint 7fl oz) ice-cold water
Lots of ice cubes

Blend the lemon juice, sugar, mint, orange blossom water (if using) and 250ml (9fl oz) of the water in a blender until green, as the chlorophyll is extracted from the mint leaves. Pour the liquid through a fine sieve and pour back into the blender. Fill a 1 litre (1¾ pint) jug with ice and add to the blender along with the remaining water. Using the ice crush function if you have it, blend the ice into a slush and pour into chilled glasses to serve.

Linden
Tilia spp.

Whether you live in an apartment in a city, in a stately home or in a cabin deep in an ancient woodland, you'll probably have linden as a neighbour. With its soft, asymmetrical heart-shaped leaves, and trunks often surrounded at the base by ruffs of suckers, linden can most easily be identified when it is in flower. If the heady, honeyed scent that surrounds the tree isn't identification enough, the hum of bees feeding from the little cream starburst-like flowers dangling from papery bracts will.

And once you inhale the scent of a linden tree, you may fall under its spell. Used in herbal medicine and aromatherapy, linden blossoms often find their way into anxiety-reducing and sleep-enhancing teas. The flowers and leaves are rich in beneficial mucilage. Used to heal skin and respiratory conditions, mucilage is a natural thickener (think of how chia seeds thicken water) and adds viscosity to a linden cocktail – perfect for sipping while sat under the bough of a tree, whether in a city, country estate or deep, dark, perfumed wood.

Edible parts: Bracts, flowers, leaf buds, leaves, inner bark, sap and seeds.

Harvesting: Harvest young leaves for teas and liqueurs from early spring, flowers from midsummer.

Pairs with: Melon, cucumber, lemon, apple, mint, lemon balm and walnut leaf.

Locations: Urban areas, parklands and ancient woodlands.

How to drink: linden

From unfurling spring buds and mature leaves, flowers bracts and even seeds, many parts of linden can be used to provide a gently soothing flavour and quality to drinks. Without any bitterness but with an extraordinary ability to create all-important mouthfeel, fresh and dried flowers and leaves are an invaluable part of a wild drinks larder.

Liqueurs: Make a linden flower liqueur by soaking the flowers in a neutral spirit for a few hours then sweeten with sugar or a light honey. You can also use the spent flowers from making linden flower cordial as they will still have a lot of flavour in them.

Cordials/syrups: Soaking linden flowers overnight in a warm syrup (with just a small amount of lemon juice) makes the most incredible cordial, every bit as rightfully prized as elderflower.

Thickeners: Linden leaves and bracts can be infused into teas to extract mucilage, a polysaccharide also found in chia and basil seeds. Dry the bracts and leaves and grind into a powder. Add the powder to cold water, leaving overnight to soak. Strain the liquid the next day and add to drinks for additional mouthfeel.

Tea: Both the flowers and bracts can be used to make tea. Linden tea is commonly drunk as a tisane in France with mint – both plants are known for their soothing, cooling and nerve-calming effects.

Fermented drinks: Linden flowers make a lovely addition to kombucha and water kefir drinks. Try adding linden flowers with strawberries to jun kombucha, which is made with green tea and sweetened with honey.

Linden cordial (sirop de tilleul)

In France, linden flowers have a delicious history of being turned into cordials and syrups. The leftover flowers are still crammed full of flavour and can be used to make a linden liqueur by soaking the sticky flowers in a neutral alcohol like vodka. Linden flower cordial has flavours of cucumber and melon and can be added to sparkling drinks, used in cocktails or just added to a gin and tonic.

MAKES 1.2 LITRES (2 PINTS)
500ml (18fl oz) water
500g (1lb 2oz) cane sugar
Juice of 2 lemons
30g (1oz) just-opened linden flowers
    cut away from the bracts

Bring the water and sugar to the boil in a saucepan, stirring until the sugar dissolves. Remove the pan from the heat and let cool for 10 minutes. Pour the lemon juice into the pan through a fine sieve to capture any chunks of lemon.

Place the flowers in a wide-necked jar and pour over the cooling syrup. Swirl the jar to make sure all the flowers are covered in the syrup, then cover and leave to infuse for 24 hours.

Pass the cordial through a sieve lined with fine muslin into a small pan. Gently bring to a simmer then transfer to a freshly sterilized bottle and seal while still hot. The cordial will keep for a few weeks in the fridge. To keep longer, pasteurize the bottle of cordial (see page 235).

Linden flower tea

Linden is wonderful by itself, but can be paired with lemon balm, nettle, rose or chamomile – all calming herbs that work well in any combination. Linden flower tea can be drunk throughout the day but makes a lovely bedtime drink for children and adults alike, especially for those who struggle to sleep.

SERVES 2
Dried linden flowers and bracts
Boiling water

When gathering linden flowers to make tea, select those that have not yet started turning brown. Snip off the flowers with the papery bracts attached. Lay them on a wire rack lined with a tea towel and place in a warm, dry spot with good air flow but away from direct sunlight. Turn the flowers twice a day, making sure to pull the flowers at the bottom of the pile to the top. After a few days, your flowers and bracts will become brittle; place them in an airtight container to store them.

To make linden tea, quarter-fill a teapot with dried flowers and bracts, then pour over just-boiled water and leave to infuse for 10 minutes before serving.

Common & black walnut
Juglans regia, J. nigra

Walnuts are large deciduous trees identified best by their aromatic and sizable compound leaves, which are made up of several sets of pointed leaflets. These leaves can be gathered when young, dried and drunk as an antioxidant herbal tea. Walnuts start life in the spring as yellow catkin-like flowers; by midsummer, they are dotted around the tree, encased in a spherical green outer husk. When walnuts ripen, the green shells split open and the pale brown walnuts fall from the tree to be harvested.

In midsummer across Europe, the newly formed green walnuts are collected early, chopped up and covered with alcohol to make infused liqueurs, wines and syrups. Traditionally harvested on St John's Day (24 June), when the nuts are still very young and haven't yet formed their shells, the walnuts can be sliced in half and you'll find a soft, almost jelly-like centre. In early autumn, when the nuts have fully ripened, harvest them when freshly fallen. Most can be dried out to store, but crack one open, and you will find it creamy and delicious – perfect for making into nut milks and sweet nut liqueurs such as Nocello.

Edible parts: Leaves, green young nuts, brown ripe nuts and sap.

Harvesting: Walnut trees provide a harvest from late winter until late autumn, starting with the sap as the tree starts to wake from its winter dormancy. The young leaves and developing nut husks can be collected in early summer and the ripe walnuts are often found around the base of the tree in the early autumn, falling as they ripen.

Pairs with: Linden, meadowsweet, lemon verbena, vanilla, lemon, cinnamon, nutmeg, coffee, clove, anise, fennel, honey, brandy, wine and vodka.

Locations: Parks, gardens and woodlands.

Caution: Avoid using if you are intolerant to tannins. Walnuts contain a chemical called juglone that can irritate skin and act as a natural dye, so wear rubber gloves and old clothes to avoid staining.

How to drink: walnut

The highly scented leaves of the walnut tree smell sweet and almost fruity; the unripe walnuts are rich in tannins and perfumed but bitter, and the ripe nuts are milky, with a hint of the bitter tannin from earlier in the year. Fresh walnut sap can be drunk, like birch sap, as a tonic.

Liqueurs: Across Europe, green walnuts are harvested to make local versions of walnut liqueur, from nocino in Italy to teufels kräuter in Germany and ratafia in Spain. The nuts are macerated in a sweetened alcohol with spices that vary from drink to drink.

Wine: With a lower ABV than liqueurs, infused fortified wines like vin de noix are made with the midsummer-harvested green nuts.

Cocktails: Walnuts make great cocktails, including a Walnut Old Fashioned, Walnut Alexander and the Walnut Pear Pie.

Cordials/syrups: Both ripe and green walnuts can be used to make syrups. Pound ripe walnuts into a sugar syrup and leave to infuse overnight. Cover green walnuts in sugar in the same way as making pine cone syrup (see page 43). Reducing the sap creates a nutty, perfumed syrup.

Tea: Walnut leaves are used in traditional herbal teas. Tannic and perfumed, they infuse into bitter teas. Cold-infused walnut leaf tea is sweet, making it with just boiled water gives a more bitter and tannic tea.

Milks: Ripe walnuts blended with water and left to soak overnight make delicious dairy-free milk alternatives.

Bitters/tinctures: Walnut leaves are frequently added to bitters to add a perfumed, tannic flavour.

Nocino

Originating in Italy, this dark bittersweet liqueur is made with green walnuts harvested in the middle of summer. You can make it with just walnuts as the flavouring, but traditional recipes also use cinnamon, nutmeg and cloves. Add flavours according to your fancy – a few coffee beans, a vanilla pod, a few star anise are all perfectly delicious infused in the drink. Should you want to add a wild flavour, try adding a handful of linden flowers, meadowsweet or sweet woodruff.

‑‑‑‑‑‑‑‑

MAKES 1.3 LITRES (2¼ PINTS)
300g (10½oz) green walnuts
4 cloves
1 cinnamon stick
¼ nutmeg, crumbled
Pared zest of 1 lemon
1 litre (1¾ pints) vodka
250ml (9fl oz) water
Sugar, light honey or maple syrup

Cut the walnuts in half and put them into a 2.5 litre (4½ pint) jar with the spices and zest. Cover the nuts and flavourings with vodka, press a wax paper disc onto the top of the liquid and seal with the lid. Leave to infuse for a month.

   Strain into a bowl, add the water then stir in your sweetener. Add it slowly, tasting for sweetness as you add more. Pour the sweetened liqueur into a sterilized bottle and leave to mature for 6 months before drinking.

Walnut eggnog

At Christmas time, many of us buy a bag of nuts in their shells – occasionally these nuts are actually cracked open and eaten but often are left and, over time, turn into mere decorations. Put them to far better use by turning them into the ultimate symbol of Christmas – eggnog.

‑‑‑‑‑‑‑‑

SERVES 2
100g (3½oz) walnuts, shelled
Pinch of salt
400ml (14fl oz) water
2 eggs, separated
4 teaspoons sugar
½ teaspoon vanilla extract
90ml (3fl oz) aged rum
Dash of bitters, such as mugwort or walnut
Ground nutmeg and cinnamon, to dust

To make walnut milk, soak the walnuts overnight in a bowl of cold water with a pinch of salt. Drain the nuts and rinse them thoroughly. Place the soaked nuts into a blender and process until they have a crumbly consistency. Add the water and blend for a few minutes until the liquid has turned cloudy. Leave the nut pulp to soak in the liquid for 30 minutes before straining through a fine muslin or jelly bag. This walnut milk can be stored in the fridge for a few days and can be used as a dairy milk alternative.

   To make eggnog, beat the egg yolks until creamy. In another bowl, whisk the egg whites with half the sugar until fluffy. Fold the yolks and whites together. In a separate bowl, stir 50ml (2fl oz) of the walnut milk with the vanilla, rum, bitters and remaining sugar until blended. Fold in the egg mix, divide between two glasses and serve dusted with nutmeg and cinnamon.

Mugwort
Artemisia vulgaris

Found growing on verges, field edges and wasteland, if you see swathes of grey feathery leaves growing on metre-high slender stems, tipped with lines of tiny furry flower buds that mature into equally small browny-red flowers, you're probably looking at mugwort. It has a gently bitter flavour with hints of mint, juniper and sage, giving it a place alongside the culinary herbs of Northern Europe and Asia, where it is added to soups, stuffings, vegetable dishes and, of course, drinks – flavouring everything from hot chocolate and warm milky drinks to wines and cocktails.

Mugwort has revered herbal properties, most importantly due to a compound called tryptophan. This amino acid stimulates the reflexes responsible for relaxing your muscles during sleep and often aids a dream-filled slumber. It is one of the key herbs included in smudge sticks, which are used to fill rooms with smouldering aromatic smoke to induce blissful dreams. For those more interested in flavour than ceremony, simply dip your smoking bundle of sticks into a sugar syrup and you'll have a smoked flavouring that is so delicious you'll think you're dreaming.

Edible parts: Leaves, stems, flower buds and flowers.

Harvesting: Gather the leaves from spring until autumn. The young shoots and unopened flower buds in spring are the most aromatic and flavoursome.

Pairs with: Fennel, anise, mint, chamomile, linden, lemon balm, rose, lavender, sage, rosemary, chocolate, milk and matcha.

Locations: Roadside verges, field margins and wasteland.

Caution: Do not use mugwort if pregnant or breastfeeding. It is not recommended for children. If you are sensitive to the properties of mugwort you might find you have very vivid dreams. Occasionally, it can cause hallucinations so introduce it in small amounts to check your sensitivity and avoid using it for a prolonged period of time.

How to drink: mugwort

Mugwort's combination of bitter, herbal, floral and sweet flavours makes it a versatile flavouring for everything from sweet comforting drinks to bitters. It is so strong, a single drop in a cocktail will work its magic.

Wine: Add mugwort to homemade versions of bitter fortified wines such as vermouth, amaro, Campari and Chartreuse.

Liqueurs: The bitter herbal taste infuses beautifully into liqueurs. Japanese drinks makers Dover make an aromatic liqueur with Japanese mugwort (known as Yomogi), which is now a staple of Japanese bars and cocktails.

Beer: Use mugwort like yarrow in herbal gruit-style ales.

Tea: Both fresh and dried mugwort make a delicious, nerve-calming tea. It is often paired with chamomile, lemon balm, rose petals, linden and mint.

Warming/milky drinks: In Korea, mugwort is harvested in the spring, dried, ground into a powder and used in drinks much like matcha. Mugwort's association with aiding sleep makes it the perfect herb to add to bedtime milky drinks, especially hot chocolate.

Fermented drinks: Mugwort leaves add a herbal flavour to health-giving fermented drinks, including ginger beer (especially lovely blended with elderflower), kombucha and water kefir drinks.

Bitters/tinctures: Mugwort is perfect for bitters; combine with other flavours such as rose petal, elderflower or chocolate.

Mugwort summer vermouth

This recipe is inspired by the flavours that are around when mugwort is at its peak – a light vermouth with a quick infusion using fresh herbs and flowers rather than dried roots or spices. Lovely drunk by itself or served in a Martini. If you want to use tougher botanicals, infuse them a few days earlier.

MAKES 750ML (1 PINT 7FL OZ)
750ml (1 pint 7fl oz) white wine
150ml (5fl oz) brandy or grappa
20g (³/₄oz) fresh mugwort (ideally picked
   when the plant is in bud)
10g (¹/₄oz) fresh yarrow
5g (¹/₈oz) fresh oregano
10g (¹/₄oz) elderflowers, or 2 tablespoons
   elderflower cordial (see page 69)
10g (¹/₄oz) rose petals
1 teaspoon lavender flowers
40g (1¹/₂oz) strawberries (preferably wild), diced
5 juniper berries, crushed
¹/₄ teaspoon chamomile tea
¹/₂ teaspoon fennel seeds
20g (³/₄oz) dandelion leaves or a 5cm (2in) piece
   of burdock leaf, chopped
4 tablespoons light honey or unrefined sugar,
   plus extra to taste

Place all ingredients in a non-reactive saucepan and heat gently until just simmering. Remove from the heat, cover and leave to infuse for at least 5 hours. Now taste; it should be floral, herbal and fruity yet pleasantly bitter, nice enough to be drunk neat over ice. If it's too bitter, add more sweetness; if not strong enough, leave to infuse more.

   When the flavour is right, strain through a sieve lined with a double layer of muslin, then again through a coffee filter. Decant into a sterilized bottle and store in the fridge, drinking within 2 months.

Mugwort & chocolate bitters

Mugwort not only pairs with milky hot chocolate, but also its more bitter version of cacao beans. Together, mugwort and cacao make the most delicious bitters to use in darker cocktails made with rum, whisky or brandy. Your Espresso Martini will thank you for a drop or two.

MAKES 150ML (5FL OZ)
175ml (6fl oz) whisky
1 tablespoon cacao nibs or very dark chocolate,
   chopped (at least 80% cacao)
15g (¹/₂oz) chopped fresh mugwort
1 teaspoon dried orange peel
¹/₄ cinnamon stick
3 cardamom pods
¹/₂ vanilla pod, split lengthways
¹/₂ teaspoon dried gentian root (optional)
¹/₂ teaspoon dried wild cherry bark (optional)

Place all the ingredients in a jar, seal with a tight-fitting lid and leave in a cupboard or dark room for 2 weeks to infuse.

   Strain through a sieve lined with a double layer of muslin or a cloth and store in a dark glass bottle with a pipette lid. This stores indefinitely.

Chamomile
Matricaria chamomilla,
Chamaemelum nobile

One of the most reached-for herbal teas, for which there are two species normally used: German chamomile (*Matricaria chamomilla*) or Roman chamomile (*Chamaemelum nobile*). Chamomile is beloved in herbal teas not only for its sweet apple-like scent but also because of the concentration of a chemical called chamazulene, which helps soothe and calm nerves. Both are easy to grow (Roman chamomile is used for chamomile lawns). Learning to identify them is important if you want to gather from the wild, especially German chamomile, which has inedible lookalikes.

Firstly, they both share the iconic herbal scent of chamomile. German chamomile is an annual that grows up to 30cm (12in) tall, with hairless, feathered, thin stems and leaves, topped with domed yellow-centred flowers and thin white outer petals. Slice a flower in half and you'll see it's hollow inside. Roman chamomile is a shorter, perennial plant with downy stems, and larger flatter flowerheads like large daisies but with longer white outer petals. It will spread like a mat across the ground, releasing its beautiful scent as you walk across it.

Edible parts: Leaves and flowers.

Harvesting: Pick the leaves from spring to autumn and the flowers in summer. German chamomile will keep flowering throughout the summer months, especially if you remove the heads. When harvesting, make sure to dry the flowers and leaves quickly and store in an airtight container in a dry place. Only pick on a dry day and discard any plants that have mildew.

Pairs with: Apple, orange, lemon, pear, strawberry, pineapple, fennel, tarragon, dill, mint, lemon balm, clover, lavender, cucumber and anise.

Locations: Field edges and verges; chamomile also thrives in domestic gardens.

Caution: Avoid large amounts of chamomile in pregnancy or if you are allergic to members of the daisy family.

How to drink: chamomile

Chamomile flowers are mild, earthy and herbal with an apple flavour. Their leaves are more bitter – perfect for using in bitter drinks. It's worth separating the flowers from the leaves to keep the sweet and bitter flavours distinct.

Wine: Steep 2 tablespoons of dried chamomile in a bottle of white wine with 3 tablespoons of vodka, the pared zest of an unwaxed orange and 1 tablespoon of honey for 2–3 hours. Strain and enjoy over ice.

Tea: The sweet flowerheads are used to make teas, both as cold and hot infusions. Fresh and dried flowers have a slightly different flavour; dried flowers have a hay-like aroma. Try mixing hot chamomile tea with apple juice for a soothing drink.

Liqueurs: Italian distillers Quaglia infuse chamomile into sweetened spirits to make a floral liqueur. Make your own using vodka, grappa or a white rum as a base and sweeten with a light honey.

Fermented drinks: Try adding a spoonful of chamomile flowers to ferments like kombuchas, ginger beer and pineapple-based tepache.

Bitters/tinctures: Chamomile bitters can be used in cocktails or more healthful teas, making a perfect digestive support.

Cordials/syrups: The flowers make a beautiful cordial: steep 2 tablespoons of dried (or 1 tablespoon of fresh) flowers in 500ml (18fl oz) of just-boiled water for 10 minutes. Strain into a pan, bring to the boil and stir in 300g (10½oz) of sugar. Once dissolved, remove from the heat and bottle. Lovely served with crushed strawberries to make a non-alcoholic summer drink.

Settle-down chamomile tea

As well as acting as a stress and anxiety reliever, chamomile is also a very gentle sedative, making it perfect to take the limelight in a night-time tea blend. This dried blend will store for up to a year, but you can also make the tea with fresh ingredients.

_____

FILLS A 250ML (9FL OZ) JAR
4 tablespoons dried chamomile flowers
1 tablespoon dried lavender flowers
4 tablespoons dried linden flowers
4 tablespoons dried lemon balm leaves
2 tablespoons dried hops
1 tablespoon dried rose petals

Place all the ingredients in a bowl and mix the herbs through each other to ensure an even blend. Spoon the herbs into a jar with an airtight lid.

To make the tea, place 1 heaped teaspoon per person in a pot and pour over a cup of just-boiled water per person. Brew for 10 minutes before straining and drinking. You can sweeten the tea with honey or apple juice; drink before bed.

Chamomile & fennel bitters

Chamomile bitters are used to support the digestion and can also be used to elevate a cocktail – a very clever concoction in a bottle.

_____

MAKES 200ML (7FL OZ)
1 tablespoon dried chamomile leaves and flowers
Pared zest of $1/2$ unwaxed lemon
$1/2$ teaspoon coriander seeds
$1/2$ teaspoon fennel seeds
$1/2$ tablespoon chopped dried burdock leaf
$1/2$ tablespoon chopped dandelion root
250ml (9fl oz) high-proof neutral spirit
  (such as Everclear)

Place all the ingredients in a jar and leave to infuse for a week before straining and bottling. To use for digestive benefits, dissolve a few drops into water and drink before a meal, or add a couple of drops to a cocktail.

Cherry
Prunus spp.

Wild cherries grow across the world, their many species bearing almond-scented blossoms in spring and sour fruits in the summer. Loved as much by birds as they are by people, it can be a challenge to beat the winged competition to the fruits. But if you manage to, there's no better way to use your pickings than to turn them into drinks – even the stones can be turned into incredible flavours (but see caution, below). Cherry blossom has a long history in Japan as a flavouring for food and drink, particularly during the cherry blossom-gazing festival of Hanami, when the flowers are soaked in salt, syrups, spirits and vinegars to extract the flavour.

Cherries range in flavour from sweet to incredibly sour, but are all full of beneficial compounds. They are rich in antioxidants and anti-inflammatories, with unusually high levels of melatonin, serotonin and tryptophan – all chemicals that help promote sleep.

Edible parts: Flowers, leaves, fruit and stones (after heating – see caution).

Harvesting: Harvest the flowers and leaves as soon as the flower buds are fully formed in early to mid spring. To have a chance of harvesting cherries in early to midsummer, look for trees with low-hanging branches on the edges of woodlands or fields.

Pairs with: Blossoms and stones: with rowan buds, green tea, raspberry, apricot, milk, chocolate, orange, cinnamon, sweet woodruff, juniper, vanilla, gin, vodka and sake. Fruits: with almond, pepper, cinnamon, peach, sage, brandy, bourbon, amaretto, kirsch, rum, vermouth, gin, vodka, sweet woodruff and meadowsweet.

Locations: Cherries grow in both open spaces and woodland.

Caution: The kernels inside cherry stones have an intense almond flavour. If you want to make use of this, you will need to make sure you dry the stones and heat them before use. This is because the scent is created by a chemical called amygdalin, which turns to cyanide if you chew and eat the raw kernel. Fortunately, the toxic potential (but not flavour) of amygdalin is halted by heat. Not all species of cherry have edible flowers and leaves, check before you use them.

How to drink: cherry

From early spring to summer, cherry trees provide wonderful ingredients for using in drinks. Collecting unopened flowers, fresh leaves and firm cherries with their stems still attached ensures you get the best out of your harvest.

Wine: Cherries make a rich, sweet wine which is perfect as a dessert wine.

Liqueurs: There aren't many spirits that don't work with cherry. In Portugal, sour cherries are macerated in a brandy spirit called aguardente with cinnamon to make ginja, an intensely flavoured cherry liquor. American black cherries are often called 'rum cherries' as they are delicious additions to spiced rums. Cherry leaves, flowers and even stones are used to flavour liqueurs; cherry blossoms are infused and distilled into sakes and gins. The bitter-sweet flowers blend beautifully with juniper.

Cordials/syrups: Cherry blossoms make delicate spring syrups. Infuse the blossoms in warm sugar syrup overnight (a sprig of rowan buds adds an extra flavour). The fruit also makes thirst-quenching cordials for soft drinks and cocktails.

Tea: Cherry fruits, blossoms and even leaves can be used to make teas. A number of tea manufacturers add cherry to their black teas, making an especially delicious iced tea. Dry a tray of your fruit in the summer to use through the winter months.

Warming/milky drinks: Cherry's sleep-enhancing compounds make it a perfect addition to another soporific, tryptophan-rich drink – milk. Add a spoonful of cherry syrup to warm milk with a few lavender flowers and sup before bed.

Vinegars: Mix cherry fruit syrup with vinegar to make delicious shrubs. Use fruit vinegar, red wine vinegar or apple cider vinegar to make this refreshing drink.

Juice: Extract the juice from cherries by using a juicer (pitting them first) or by placing them in a heavy-based saucepan with a splash of water. Cover and heat gently until they collapse and release their juice into the pan.

Cherry stone extract

Rather than throwing away cherry stones, let them dry out thoroughly. Come the end of the cherry-eating season, you'll have enough stones to make this unique flavouring for drinks, akin to amaretto and kirsch. You can wash any leftover cherry flesh from the stones, but leaving it to dry on the stones gives the liqueur a gentle cherry fruit flavour.

_____

MAKES 250ML (9FL OZ)
100g (3½oz) dried cherry stones
250ml (9fl oz) neutral spirit, such as vodka

Using a hammer, break open the dried stones to expose the kernels inside. Lay the cracked stones on a baking tray and place in a preheated oven at 150°C (300°F), Gas Mark 2, for 15 minutes.

Spoon the heated stones into a jar and cover with the spirit. Leave to infuse for 1 month.

Strain the liquid through a fine sieve into a sterilized dropper bottle and store for up to a year. Even just a few drops will add a nutty almond flavour to drinks and food.

Cherry, tea & meadowsweet sour

Cherries ripen just as meadowsweet flowers burst open, both with almond flavours. They're a perfectly timed flavour pairing. The addition of tea to the drink highlights the tannins in the fruit, making an almost wine-flavoured drink.

_____

SERVES 2
1 heaped teaspoon black tea
½ teaspoon dried meadowsweet
1 heaped teaspoon light brown sugar
200ml (7fl oz) boiling water
150ml (5fl oz) sour cherry juice
1 egg white
Ice cubes
2 maraschino cherries or meadowsweet sprigs,
   to decorate

Place the tea, meadowsweet and sugar in a small teapot, pour over the just-boiled water and leave to brew for 10 minutes.

Strain the tea into a cocktail shaker and add the cherry juice and egg white. Shake until the white becomes foamy. Fill the shaker with ice cubes and shake until the outside of the shaker becomes frosted. Pour the drink through a strainer into two cocktail coupes and serve decorated with maraschino cherries or sprigs of meadowsweet. (Remind yourself this isn't alcoholic.)

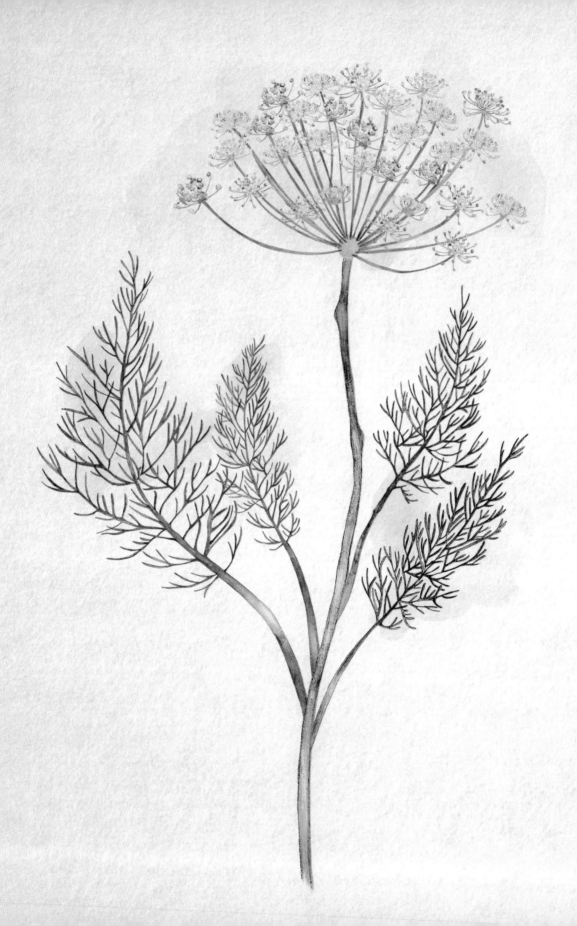

Wild fennel
Foeniculum vulgare

Wild fennel grows on road verges, in coastal areas and on wastelands, thriving on the stony ground and growing into larger clumps with each passing year. Each spring, clusters of new feathery frond-like leaves grow from the plant's gnarly roots, followed by slender, hairless, green-grey main stems that reach up to 1.8m (6ft) and side shoots with large, very fine frond-like leaves that resemble dill, a relative in the carrot family.

In late summer, fennel plants are crowned with umbels of delicate yellow flowers, which eventually turn into aromatic and aniseed-flavoured seeds. These seeds have a long association with being eaten and drunk. In fact, if you had colic as a baby, there's a good chance you were given fennel seed-infused water – otherwise known as gripe water. The ancient civilizations of Rome, Greece and Egypt all made good use of fennel, which thrives in the Mediterranean climate, and drank fennel seed tea for a plethora of health conditions including, of course, aiding digestion.

Edible parts: Frond-like leaves, stems, flowers and seeds.

Harvesting: Start picking the shoots in spring until winter, when the stalks turn brown. Gather leaves sparingly, leaving some growth to produce flowering stems. Collect the flowers by pulling off the umbels and placing into a container to avoid losing any pollen. Only take a small amount. Pick the seeds when they have just formed for the best flavour. In the winter, when the plant is dying back, the hollow stems still provide flavour; smash them with a mallet to break them open.

Pairs with: Nettle, mint, pine, rose, cucumber, elderflower, celery, rhubarb, lemon, blackcurrant, Campari and gin.

Locations: Coastal areas, road verges and wasteland.

Caution: Fennel is part of the carrot family, which includes some extremely toxic plants – most notably hemlock and hemlock water dropwort. Always take care when harvesting carrot family members, especially when you're picking the fronds in the spring, as hemlock frequently grows in the same environment as fennel. If in doubt, plant some in your garden to use.

How to drink: fennel

Young fronds of fennel have an anise flavour with a hint of mint, the yellow flowers are sweet and light, the seeds incredibly liquoriced. Even the drying stems hold a woody flavour and can be soaked in liqueurs or hot blackcurrant drinks.

Liqueurs: Fennel is one of the traditional ingredients in absinthe along with wormwood, hyssop and star anise. Fennel seeds make great-tasting liqueurs, for example, in the Italian liqueur finocchietto.

Cocktails: Fennel is a cocktail-maker's friend, working in everything from a Martini, Campari drink, Pisco or whisky – a splash of fennel syrup in an Old Fashioned will convert the most devout of sceptics.

Cordials/syrups: Made from either the fronds or seeds, fennel syrup tastes like aniseed and is a great sweetener for cocktails and non-alcoholic drinks. Try pairing it with lemon and mint to make a Greek-inspired cooler (with a splash of ouzo).

Salts/sugars: Grind fennel leaves with grapefruit zest into a good sea or kosher salt to make a delicious salt for the best Martinis.

Tea: All above-ground parts of fennel can be used as a tea. In the spring, the young fronds are lovely paired with mint and lemon balm in a cold, overnight-infused tea. The seeds are traditionally infused with honey and orange for digestion. Fennel is also delicious and digestion-aiding with ginger and lemon, mint, rose or even cinnamon.

Fermented drinks: Blend fennel with cucumber and orange peel to ferment into kvass-style drinks. Fennel is also lovely in water kefir drinks – add fennel flowers, young seeds or leaves at second fermentation with lemon for a vibrant cooler.

Bitters/tinctures: Pair fennel seeds with lemon peel, chamomile and burdock or artichoke leaves to make the ultimate digestive, health-supporting bitters.

Fennel, cardamom & rose sharbat

Fennel seeds are often added to sharbats. Similar to juleps, they are popular beverages in the Middle East and India, traditionally drunk for their hydrating and cooling qualities on hot summer days.

MAKES 500ML (18FL OZ)
1 tablespoon fennel seeds
10 cardamom pods
250ml (9fl oz) water
200g (7oz) sugar
15g (½oz) fragrant rose petals,
    or 1 teaspoon rose water

Soak the fennel seeds and cardamom overnight in the water. The next day, grind the mixture in a blender, then pour through a fine sieve lined with muslin into a saucepan. Add 125ml (4fl oz) more water and the sugar. Heat, stirring, until the sugar has dissolved, then simmer for 10 minutes or until it thickens slightly.

Take the pan off the heat and add the rose petals or rose water. If you are using petals, allow them to infuse for 30 minutes, before straining the liquid and transferring to freshly sterilized bottles. It can be stored in the fridge for up to 2–3 months.

To serve, pour 1 tablespoon of the syrup into a glass with lemon juice to taste. Drop in a few fennel fronds and rose petals before adding ice cubes. Top up with water or soda water, stir to mix the syrup and serve.

Apple & fennel cocktail

Freshly juiced apples and fennel fronds make a cocktail that is so full of vitality it's practically good for you. If you don't add gin, it really is. Quite how good you want to be is up to you but, rest assured, this is delicious either way.

SERVES 2
2 young fennel fronds and stems, around
    15cm (6in) long
2 green cooking apples, halved and cored
    (leave the skin on)
4 tablespoons gin
1 tablespoon simple sugar syrup
10 mint leaves
Dash of bitters (fennel bitters would be perfect)
Pinch of salt (fennel and grapefruit salt if you
    have it)
Fennel flowers, to decorate
Crushed ice, to serve

Juice the fennel and apples – if you don't have a juicer, blend them in a food processor with the gin and syrup then strain through a fine sieve. Pour the juice, gin, syrup, mint leaves and bitters into a chilled cocktail shaker with a cup of ice. Shake, then divide the drink between two tumblers filled with ice. Top with a pinch of salt and decorate with fennel flowers.

Rosebay willow herb
Chamaenerion angustifolium

Tall swathes of rosebay willow herb start to flower in the middle of summer, the bright pink flowers with blue pollen slowly progressing up their slender stems, leaving long seed pods once the flowers finish their display. In some areas of Scotland, rosebay willow herb is known as 'summer's candle' because the further up the plant the flowers bloom, the closer it is to the end of summer. Coincidentally, the seed pods burst open when mature, releasing a huge amount of fluffy seed which can be used as a tinder to light fires. In North America, Canada and parts of Europe, the plant is known as 'fireweed' because it thrives in areas where there have been fires, often covering burned forests and clearfell sites with large expanses of pink.

Rosebay also provides medicinal properties – it is anti-inflammatory, lowers cholesterol and is rich in vitamins C and A. When used in drinks it tastes fruity and rather like cranberries. That might all be enough to make you want to head out to gather the plant, but rosebay willow herb has one last party trick – its flowers are pH indicators and when you add acidity from lemon juice, for example, your drink will not only taste delicious and fruity, but will turn bright pink, as pink as its flowers.

Edible parts: Shoots, leaves and flowers.

Harvesting: If you pick the leaves before flowering, avoid pulling away the buds that are forming along the stems. When harvesting the flowers in summer, pick small amounts from a wide area as they are an important food source for pollinators.

Pairs with: Yarrow, meadowsweet, rosemary, tea, ginger, honey, redcurrant, apple, lemon, gin, vodka and mead.

Locations: Woodland clearings, roadsides and marginal areas.

Note: Don't be tempted to harvest lengths of flowering stem unless you can process them quickly – the flowers rapidly turn to seed and your harvest (and kitchen) will become full of the fluffy seedheads.

How to drink: rosebay willow herb

Rosebay willow herb is so beneficial that it's well worth harvesting enough to preserve for the winter months.

Wine: Rosebay willow herb flowers make delicious floral wines and meads. Should you have access to rosebay willow herb honey, use this in the mead.

Liqueurs: Estonian distillery Surakas make Rüübe vodka flavoured with the flowers to add an aromatic and rounded taste. Try making a rosebay willow herb liqueur by macerating fresh or dried flowers in vodka for a few hours (or overnight if using dried flowers) and sweeten with honey.

Cordials/syrups: Bright pink rosebay willow herb cordial is astringent and fruity, delicious with water or tonic (with or without gin).

Tea: The leaves and flowers are both used in herbal teas. Freshly picked leaves have a long tradition of being made into a black tea by rolling them until they wilt and pushing them into a jar for a couple of days to start fermenting. Once they start smelling fruity, almost like red wine, they are laid out to dry then stored in airtight containers. The herbal tea is rich in vitamin C, magnesium and B vitamins, and is thought to support heart and prostate health.

Fermented drinks: Rosebay willow herb leaves and flowers are delicious used in probiotic ferments; try adding flowers to a ginger beer or kefir. The tannic leaves are perfect in kombuchas.

Bitters/tinctures: Canadian bitters makers Free Pour Jenny's blend rosebay willow herb flowers with spices including green cardamom to make their Fireweed Bitters.

Rosebay willow herb kombucha

Pairing the two giants of fermented tea, camellia and rosebay willow herb, in a kombucha makes a fruity and astringent drink. You can either use fresh leaves and flowers or fermented ones for a stronger, more tannic, flavour.

MAKES 2 LITRES (3¹/₂ PINTS)
2 litres (3¹/₂ pints) water
2 teaspoons organic black tea
150g (5oz) granulated sugar
1 kombucha SCOBY, plus 100ml (3¹/₂fl oz) retained
    liquid from the previous first ferment
20g (³/₄oz) fresh or 10g (¹/₄oz) dried rosebay willow
    herb flowers and leaves

Heat the water in a saucepan until just boiled, turn off the heat and add the tea and sugar. Stir until the sugar has dissolved then leave for 10 minutes to infuse. Strain out the tea and leave to cool.

Place the SCOBY and its liquid into a sterilized 2 litre (3¹/₂ pint) jar and top up with the sweetened tea, leaving a 5cm (2in) gap at the top of the jar. Cover with a clean cloth, secure with a band, and leave to ferment for at least 7 days at room temperature away from direct sunlight.

When the first fermentation is complete, taste the kombucha – it should be pleasantly acidic and sharp. Once it is, remove the SCOBY and pour the liquid into a sterilized wide-necked jar with a tight seal (or two smaller jars). Add the rosebay willow herb, make sure it is submerged and seal for a few days to infuse the flavour and increase carbonation. Once fizzy, strain into a bottle and store in the fridge for up to 30 days, opening the lid occasionally to release excess pressure.

Rosebay willow herb cordial

Rosebay willow herb's bright pink flowers are – like violet, nettle and rose petals – pH indicators. The lemon juice in this recipe not only balances the flower's astringent flavours but also turns the cordial bright pink. Delicious served as a soft drink or as a mixer for a gin and soda.

MAKES 650ML (1 PINT 2FL OZ)
500ml (18fl oz) boiling water
50g (2oz) rosebay willow herb flowers
300g (10¹/₂oz) sugar
Juice of 3 lemons

Pour 300ml (¹/₂ pint) of the just-boiled water over the flowers, push all the flowers under the water, cover and leave to infuse for 30 minutes or until the flowers have lost their colour.

Pour the remaining water into a saucepan and bring to a simmer. Add the sugar and heat, stirring, until it has dissolved and the liquid has become clear. Strain the infused water into the syrup and stir.

Pass the lemon juice through a fine sieve into the cordial (oohhing and aahhing as it turns bright pink). Pour into sterilized bottles and store in the fridge for up to 2 months. Serve with sparkling water or splashed into a gin and tonic.

Wild thyme
Thymus spp.

Thymes are tough, low-growing subshrubs that can be found in locations as diverse as hot, dry Mediterranean rocks, windswept chalky cliffs or high bleak moorland. However, you're probably more likely to have come across thymes in gardens or the herb section of the supermarket. What rarely make it into a packet of herbs are its small purple, pink or magenta flowers which burst into bloom through the summer. This is a shame, because thyme flowers offer their own sweeter, honeyed flavour distinct from the herbal, earthy and almost citrus perfume of the leaves.

In ancient Greece, thyme was seen as a plant that would give athletes staying power and soldiers courage. Perhaps they were inspired by its fortitude – growing where other more fragile, weaker plants could not. It wasn't the ancient Greeks who first started admiring thyme, though. Way back in Sumeria in 2750BC, a recipe for a poultice made from dried thyme, figs and pears was inscribed onto a tablet. It sounds more like a cocktail than a cure – perhaps it was made by the first mixologist herbalist? It's well worth raising a glass up (or rather down) to this aromatic herb.

Edible parts: Leaves, stems and flowers.

Harvesting: Harvest wild and cultivated thymes with scissors, trimming off the top growth, but leaving stems with leaves still on to allow the plant to regenerate. Harvest foliage all year round, and the flowers in midsummer to early autumn.

Pairs with: Lavender, mint, fennel, anise, rosemary, sage, blueberry, elderberry, pear, apple, lemon, orange, fig, white wine, vodka, whisky, rum, vermouth, Negronis and arak.

Locations: Hillsides, rocky areas, coastal paths and herb gardens.

Caution: Avoid large amounts of thyme if you are pregnant.

How to drink: thyme

Thyme's aromatic, deep flavour makes it a wonderful herb to use in wild drinks. Dried thyme has a different flavour to fresh, becoming more intense as it dries. Use a teaspoon of dried thyme for every three of fresh.

Wine: In France, dry white wines are infused with thyme and honey to make an elegant aperitif.

Liqueurs: Use to infuse into gins, sweetened neutral spirits like schnapps and vodka, and stronger-flavoured spirits like arak (a Middle Eastern drink akin to ouzo, made with anise).

Distilled drinks: Thyme water is produced as a by-product of distilling the essential oil and makes a useful flavouring – add to water for a uniquely herbal drink; it's also lovely used with whisky, or as an ingredient in cocktails.

Cordials/syrups: Infuse fresh or dried thyme in a sugar syrup with a twist of lemon zest and add to pomegranate juice to make a non-alcoholic cocktail that will make drinkers jealous.

Tea: Thyme flowers and leaves have a long history of being drunk as a medicinal tea to treat viruses and respiratory conditions, among other ailments. Thyme is often blended with other herbs such as yarrow and rosemary, but can be brewed with black tea leaves.

Fermented drinks: Thyme is a traditional ingredient in mead; if you can find thyme honey, use that as well to push thyme to the centre of the drink.

Salts/sugars: Finely powder dried thyme flowers and leaves with salt to make a beautiful pink finishing salt for the best dressed (and flavoured) Martinis.

Thyme, pear & fig healer

Inspired by Sumerian medics, this combination of thyme, pear and fig creates a deliciously fruity, herbal and sour non-alcoholic cocktail. Should you need fortifying with a medicinal alcoholic spirit, add a measure of brandy to the drink. The doctor would approve.

————

SERVES 2
1 ripe fig
5 thyme sprigs, plus extra to decorate
2 tablespoons lemon juice
300ml (½ pint) pear juice
Dash of bitters
Ice cubes
Soda water

Slice the fig in half, place it with the thyme in a cocktail shaker and use a muddling stick to crush the fig with the thyme. Add the lemon and pear juice along with a dash of bitters and muddle again before sealing and shaking the drink. Strain into two tumblers filled with ice and top up with soda water. Decorate with thyme sprigs.

Thyme aperitif

Thyme flowers' delicate and floral flavours transfer into sweetened wine to make a lightly infused aperitif; serve over ice, under shade.

————

MAKES 750ML (1 PINT 7FL OZ)
1 bottle dry white wine
4 tablespoons light honey
60ml (2fl oz) eau de vie or vodka
10 flowering thyme sprigs, freshly harvested,
    plus extra to decorate

Remove around 125ml (4fl oz) of wine from the bottle (which just so happens to be a small glass). Warm the honey until it becomes liquid and pour into the bottle of wine. Add the spirit and push the flowering thyme stems into the bottle. Seal, and leave to infuse for 24 hours before straining. Serve chilled over ice as an aperitif with a sprig of thyme to decorate.

Yarrow
Achillea millefolium

If you crouch down and take a look at a patch of grass, you'll most likely find some yarrow in there too, one of the most common grassland plants on the planet. It grows in a mat with finely divided leaves resembling feathery ferns and, if you let your patch of grass grow, by late summer, your knee-high lawn would be covered in downy, silvery flowering stems topped with creamy white flowerheads, the clusters of little flowers dusted in yellow pollen when they open.

Yarrow is related to chamomile and, like chamomile, it has a combination of bitter and sweet flavours – most definitely herbal, with hints of tarragon in its delicate leaves. It is renowned as an incredible medicinal herb and has made its way into drinks because of these properties. Used by herbalists for everything from healing skin conditions to balancing hormones and stopping bleeding, it's no wonder yarrow was included in early medicinal ales. The flowers and leaves are used to this day to flavour bitters and liqueurs, but now more often for their fortifying rather than their medicinal qualities (but no one will judge you if you pretend to be sipping yarrow vermouth for its healing effects).

Edible parts: Feathery leaves, flowers, stems and roots.

Harvesting: From mid spring until late autumn. Flowers are the most potently flavoured part of the plant.

Pairs with: Tarragon, chervil, sage, oregano, ginger, elderflower, lemon, grapefruit, orange, blackberry, pear, apple and rosehip.

Locations: Grasslands – lawns, meadows and verges.

Caution: Avoid yarrow if you are pregnant, breastfeeding or on blood-thinning medication.

How to drink: yarrow

Yarrow can add a unique flavour to drinks. The bitter compounds combined with floral perfumes add a distinctive taste to everything from teas to liqueurs.

 Beer: Yarrow has a long history of being used in beers and ales and is one of the ingredients in herbal ales called gruits. Use yarrow as a bittering agent in herbal ales and beers made with grains, in place of or alongside hops.

 Liqueurs: Yarrow flowers and leaves infused into neutral spirits create a fresh, astringent drink with a slightly thymol, camphor flavour. Finnish distillery Koskenkorva makes yarrow, lemon and lime vodka, a herbal, citrusy drink.

 Cordials/syrups: Yarrow infused in sugar syrup makes a tonic-like syrup – bitter, sweet and herbal. Pour hot sugar syrup over freshly opened flowers and leaves and leave to stand overnight before sieving and bottling. Yarrow syrup is lovely added to fruit juice to make mocktails with an adult flavour, or used in place of tonic.

 Tea: Both the leaves, stems and flowers can be made into teas. Yarrow dies back in the winter so dry and store a supply to help fight winter viruses.

 Bitters/tinctures: The bitter compounds in yarrow make it an ideal bitters ingredient. Use all parts of the plant, including the flowers, leaves and roots. Yarrow bitters are especially delicious in herbal cocktails.

 Salts/sugars: Yarrow salt gives a deep, final flavour to cocktails and mocktails.

Yarrow & lemon zest gin

Yarrow features in many craft gins for good reason, adding an astringent, earthy and herbal flavour to the drink. This recipe boosts the yarrow flavour with the addition of lemon zest, making an already good bottle very good indeed.

——————

MAKES 700ML (1¼ PINTS)
500ml (18fl oz) gin
15g (½oz) yarrow flowers and leaves
Pared zest of 2 unwaxed lemons
60g (2oz) granulated sugar

Pour the gin over the yarrow flowers in a large jug, ensuring the flowers are completely covered. Then set aside.

   Place the lemon zest in a large bowl with the sugar, and rub the sugar into the zest. Ensuring the zest is covered in sugar, leave for 4–5 hours, during which time the sugar will draw out the oils.

   Stain the infused gin over the lemon zest mixture and stir to make sure the lemon oils dissolve into the gin. Strain the gin through a muslin-lined sieve into a sterilized bottle. Serve neat over ice or with tonic. This can be stored for up to a year.

Chilled rosebay willow herb & yarrow tea

Rosebay willow herb and yarrow flower through the summer and the flavours are delicious together in this thirst-quenching tea. This drink is unapologetically astringent – if you would like to sweeten it, add a spoonful of sugar or light honey.

——————

SERVES 4
5 yarrow flowerheads
10g (¼oz) rosebay willow herb flowers
300ml (½ pint) boiling water
Juice of 1 lemon
500ml (18fl oz) chilled water
Ice cubes, to serve

Place the yarrow and rosebay willow herb flowers in a teapot and pour over the just-boiled water. Cover and leave to brew for 10 minutes. Pour the tea into a jug and stir in the lemon juice and chilled water. Serve with ice cubes.

Autumn

Autumn's lengthening shadows and shortening days remind us that it will soon be time to head indoors to curl up and hibernate. Its bounty of richly flavoured and nutritionally laden fruits and nuts make this a busy time in kitchens – cooking fruit into cordials, piecing their skins to be soaked in alcohol to make warming liqueurs, and storing nuts for the lean months ahead. Preserving the abundance now will provide you with a delicious store of tipples to sip through the cold days to come.

Blackberry
Rubus fruticosus

Take a walk on a late summer's day down any road, lane or alleyway and you'll probably come across blackberries, also known as brambles, with their thorny, woody stems, prickly, palmate leaves and berries that ripen from the end of each cluster, working inwards. Look for the berries at the tips if you want sweetness, further along for sour. If your sour taste buds are particularly strong, collect the fully formed but still red, hard berries to blend and make a delicious liquid – bramble verjus – which is as sour as lemons, the perfect souring agent for autumnal cocktails and mocktails.

It's not just in late summer and autumn that you can harvest from brambles. In the early spring, the young leaf buds start growing. A nibble on a bud will first taste astringent, but after a few moments will change quite miraculously to coconut – a lot like the way gorse flowers smell and taste in the warm sun. Bramble leaf buds and leaves are rich in tannins and compounds that settle upset stomachs. Steeped in hot water, they make delicious, comforting tea.

Edible parts: Leaf buds, leaves, new shoots, flowers and berries.

Harvesting: Collect leaf buds in spring and leaves during the spring, summer and autumn months. The berries can hang onto their briars for months after they have ripened. Aim to harvest the berries when they are at their peak – at the end of summer or the start of autumn. After the autumn equinox, they are less likely to ripen and those that do are more likely to be insipid – avoid any that are squishy.

Pairs with: Whisky, apple, brandy, ginger, vanilla, honey, lemon, basil, thyme, mint, star anise and cinnamon.

Locations: Hedgerows, thickets and scrubland.

Caution: Brambles are very thorny and send down thick vines into the ground. When gathering brambles, wear long trousers and sturdy shoes! Avoid bramble leaves during pregnancy.

How to drink: blackberry

Early spring brings swelling leaf buds that taste of coconut, followed by leaves rich in tannins. Finally, the dark fruits swell, themselves with a hint of coconut. They are delicious in coconut drinks such as Piña Colada or coconut milkshakes.

Wine: Blackberry wine is considered one of the finest fruit wines. Use some leaves with the fruit to add tannins.

Liqueurs: Bramble liqueurs can be made by simply soaking the fruit in spirits (in the same way as Sloe gin, see page 187) or by reducing the juice into fortified wine (see Crème de mûre, opposite). Because bramble's sweetness is very variable, sweeten after straining the fruit. Brambles pair with most spirits, from whisky and dark spiced rum to gin. Infuse bramble leaf buds with gorse flowers in a white rum to impart coconut flavour to the spirit.

Cordials/syrups: Select sour brambles to make fruit cordials, adding a handful of elderberries or plums for a rounded flavour.

Tea: Bramble leaves make a soothing vitamin C-rich tea that is used in herbal treatments for sore throats and gums, as well as gastrointestinal illnesses. The leaves can be used fresh, dried or fermented (like the Rosebay willow herb kombucha on page 129). Try smashing blackberries with mint into iced tea for a fruity drink.

Fermented drinks: Blackberries make fantastic wild sodas and flavoured kombuchas (added at the second fermentation). Try adding beetroot with blackberries to make fruity kvass-style drinks.

Vinegars: Blackberry vinegars make delicious shrubs – pair them with thyme or lavender for a herbal flavour.

Juice: Either press the berries through a sieve or use a juicer. Pair blackberries with apples to make a fruit drink. Unripe blackberries produce a sour juice known as verjus, which makes a wonderful souring ingredient in cocktails.

Crème de mûre

Crème de mûre is an unapologetically sweet drink. Created in 19th-century France, its almost jammy flavour makes it a cross between a syrup and a liqueur. This version of the tipple has less sugar than traditional recipes – if you want to take it back to the original cloying levels, double the amount of sugar.

MAKES 1 LITRE (1³/₄ PINTS)
500g (1lb 2oz) blackberries
1 bottle of red wine
250g (9oz) sugar
250ml (9fl oz) vodka

Place the blackberries in a bowl and mash them with a fork to break them up. Pour over the red wine, cover and leave to macerate for 2 days.

Strain the berry-infused wine through a sieve, pressing out as much liquid as possible. Strain the liquid again, this time though a muslin-lined sieve or jelly bag, without squeezing the pulp, to capture the clear juice. Pour the juice into a saucepan and add the sugar. Bring the liquid to a simmer, stirring until the sugar has dissolved, then simmer very gently for 10 minutes to reduce it. Remove from the heat and allow to cool.

Add the vodka to the wine and transfer to freshly sterilized bottles. Store for up to 1 year; drink within 6 months of opening.

Turn your crème de mûre into a classic bramble cocktail by shaking 50ml (2fl oz) of gin, 25ml (1fl oz) of lemon juice (or blackberry verjus) and ¹/₂ tablespoon of simple sugar syrup with ice in a cocktail shaker. Strain into a cocktail glass over crushed ice, drizzle over 1 tablespoon of the crème de mûre, pop a blackberry on top and serve.

Blackberry switchel

Blackberries and thyme both blend beautifully with each other, and ginger, making them an ideal trio in thirst-quenching, vinegar-based switchels. If you happen upon some elderberries on your foray for blackberries, substituting 50g (2oz) of the blackberries with elderberries will add even more flavour, making a happy trio an ecstatic quartet.

MAKES 1 LITRE (1³/₄ PINTS)
30ml (1fl oz) honey
30ml (1fl oz) apple cider vinegar
10g (¹/₄oz) grated ginger
150g (5oz) blackberries
1 teaspoon chopped thyme
1 litre (1³/₄ pints) still or sparkling water

Place the honey, vinegar, ginger and blackberries in a saucepan and, over a low heat, stir until the honey has dissolved and the blackberries have collapsed. Add the thyme and leave to infuse for 30 minutes before pressing through a sieve.

Once cooled, dilute with 1 litre (1³/₄ pints) of still or sparkling water and serve over ice. If you don't use all the base mixture, it can be stored in the fridge for up to 4 weeks.

Sumac
Rhus spp.

Sumac is best known as a spice made by grinding up the berries of the rhus tree, which adds a sharp, fruity, tannic flavour to Middle Eastern dishes. The taste comes from the water-soluble malic acid that coats the berries as they ripen in late summer and early autumn. Sumac berries grow in clusters known as drupes or bobs, which sit on the ends of the branches, facing upwards, like light bulbs on a chandelier. There are a number of different species of edible sumac and, according to where you are, your local sumac might be smooth sumac (*Rhus glabra*), staghorn sumac (*R. typhina*), with its velvety branches and berries, or Sicilian sumac (*R. coriaria*), which grows across the Middle East and is the main source of the spice.

But it's not just in the Middle East that sumac is used. In America, the water-soluble berries have been used for thousands of years as a medicinal, thirst-quenching drink. This is made by simply soaking them in water to release their flavour and beneficial properties, which include antioxidant vitamins A and C, metabolic-supporting B vitamins, tannins and heart-supporting compounds. With all its health benefits as well as a sharp, fruity flavour, sumac should perhaps be found as often in the drinks cupboard as it is in the spice rack.

Edible parts: Berries and young shoots.

Harvesting: The berries ripen at the end of the summer; pick when they are bright red. The flavours are water soluble and will wash off the berries in rain, so harvest after a few days of dry weather. Dry the berries in a dehydrator or low oven for a few hours, crumble and store whole or ground into a powder. The seeds are edible but can be sieved out to make a finer powder.

Pairs with: Rosehip, blackberry, elderberry, ginger, saffron, cardamom, rose, orange, melon, black tea, vinegar, vodka and tequila.

Locations: Marginal scrubland and gardens.

Caution: Sumac is related to cashew and some people are allergic to both. There are some trees known as 'sumacs' that are toxic (including the poison sumac). Edible sumacs have red clusters of upward-facing berries.

How to drink: sumac

Sumac's sour fruity flavour makes a delicious ingredient in drinks, whether it's used fresh or dried. You can infuse whole drupes or pulled-apart berries into drinks – whole drupes have more of an astringent taste from the woody stem.

Wine: Sumac ferments into a citrusy fresh wine that is ideal drunk young.

Beer: Sumac ripens at the same time as hops – adding fresh sumac to hoppy brews adds a clean, sharp flavour to beer. Iranian-American brewers Back Home Beer add sumac to their brews to make a gose beer, giving the beer hints of sour cherry.

Liqueurs: Sumac is delicious infused into spirits such as vodka and tequila, either alone or with orange.

Cordials/syrups: Sumac cordial is fruity and astringent, perfect for adding to soft drinks or cocktails. Make a syrup by infusing the berries in hot water for a couple of hours, then strain and place in a saucepan with 400g (14oz) of sugar for every 500ml (18fl oz) of liquid; simmer, stirring until the sugar has dissolved. Try adding the orange zest to the infusion.

Tea: Sumac berries make a lovely fruity drink, either by themselves or paired with rosehips, elderberries or blackberries in a hot or chilled tea.

Fermented drinks: Add sumac to ginger beer; tannin-rich sumac leaves can also be added to kombuchas.

Vinegars: Infuse sumac berries into apple cider vinegar or red wine vinegar and sweeten with honey or sugar to make a sweet-sour drinking vinegar.

Salts/sugars: The sharp flavour is an ideal contrast to salt or sugar for finishing cocktails. Either blend dried berries with salt or sugar to make a fine powder, or blend the ingredients with a splash of water in a mini blender to make a paste. This will pull out the vibrant colour of the sumac into the salt or sugar. Spread on baking paper and dry before storing in a jar for up to a year.

Sumac water kefir

Sumac adds a delicious flavour and nutritional boost to fermented drinks. Water kefir is a probiotic drink made by using kefir grains (clusters of beneficial bacteria). It's also lovely with rosehips, blackberries or elderberries. If you add elderberries, cook them first to make them safe to eat.

MAKES 500ML (18FL OZ)
20g (³/₄oz) water kefir grains
750ml (1 pint 7fl oz) unchlorinated water
35g (1¹/₄oz) sugar
1 tablespoon whole sumac berries,
   or 1 teaspoon ground

If the water kefir grains are new, activate them first by placing in a jug with 250ml (9fl oz) of unchlorinated water and 15g (¹/₂oz) of sugar. Stir, cover and leave at room temperature out of direct sunlight for 48 hours. Drain the grains and discard the water.

Place the activated grains in a jar with another 15g (¹/₂oz) sugar and the remaining 500ml (18fl oz) of unchlorinated water. Cover the jar with a clean cloth and secure with a rubber band or a preserving jar ring. Leave at room temperature out of direct sunlight for 48 hours (or longer if in a cold room).

Strain the grains and pour the liquid into a sterilized bottle with the sumac berries and remaining 5g (¹/₈oz) sugar. Seal and leave to ferment for 3–5 days until the liquid is effervescent. Again, if it is cold this process might take longer, up to 10 days. Every few days, gently open the lid to release pressure and check for carbonation. Once fizzy, drink straight away or store in the fridge for up to a month, regularly opening the lid to prevent the pressure from building up too much.

Sumacade

In both the Mediterranean and North America, sumac's incredible water-soluble ability has been put to good use for hundreds, if not thousands, of years to make one of the easiest sour, fruity and cooling drinks that is packed full of nutritional benefits.

MAKES 1 LITRE (1³/₄ PINTS)
2 drupes of sumac berries
1 litre (1³/₄ pints) water
Sugar or blackberries (optional)

Plunge the whole drupes into a jug or pull the berries from the main stem first – leaving the berries attached to the main stem will make them easier to remove, but the stem will add a more woody, astringent flavour. Cover and leave to infuse out of direct sunlight for at least 12 hours before straining through a fine sieve. Serve as it is, or sweeten with sugar or a few smashed sweet blackberries.

Elder (berry)
Sambucus nigra

Back in the warm days of early summer elder trees were covered in their creamy flowers but now is the time to head back to those wise old elders for their second harvest, because the flowers you didn't gather in the summer will now have turned into large clusters of round, almost black berries. Rich in vitamin C and anthocyanins, elderberries are both nutritious and renowned for their health-supporting benefits. Just as elderflowers offer the perfect combination of summer curative properties – cooling, anti-inflammatory, decongestant and antiviral – elderberries have a long history of being used to fight cold and flu viruses and boost the immune system.

For all the benefits elderberries bring you, don't be tempted to graze on the raw berries – elderberries need heating or fermenting to make them safe to eat. They will then be safe to consume, but not yet delicious. Because elderberries are unusually low in acidity and sugars, they are best paired with a fruitier, more acidic counterpart such as apple juice, blackcurrants, lemons or wine to make the fruit taste good enough to drink – proving the adage that a spoonful of sugar really does help the medicine go down.

Edible parts: Flowers in early summer and berries in early autumn.

Harvesting: Elderberries are ripe when they are dark, glossy and soft. Occasionally you'll find whole clusters of berries all ripe at the same time; snip the whole cluster away from the tree and, using a fork or your fingers, pull the berries off their stems into a container. If some of the berries aren't ripe, leave the cluster on the tree and pick off the ripe berries one by one.

Pairs with: Apple, blackcurrant, elderflower, honeysuckle, rose, lemon, red wine, port, cider, vinegar, rum, vodka, pineapple weed, cinnamon, clove, star anise and thyme.

Locations: Hedgerows, woodland edges and gardens.

Caution: Elderberries must be cooked or fermented to be safe to eat. The flowers and berries are the only edible parts of the elder.

How to drink: elderberry

Elderberries are often paired with acidic fruits for good reason – they are very low in acid and sugar so they need an acidic fruit partner to make their flavour shine. If you want to store elderberries before you use them, dry them in a dehydrator or freeze them in tubs and scoop out the berries as you need them.

Wine: Elderberries make outstanding red wines, tasting almost as rich as port. Due to their low acidity and sugars, you will need to add both acid and sweetness to your brew.

Liqueurs: Elderberries are lovely infused into wines and spirits. In France, elderberries are made into vin de grape du sureau, blending the berries with white wine, brandy and sugar.

Cordials/syrups: Blending elderberries with apples, blackcurrants or elderflowers and lemons turns them into a cordial that can be enjoyed chilled in soft drinks and cocktails or hot in apple juice or mulled drinks such as Scandinavian glögg.

Tea: Dried elderberries paired with dried rosehips and hawthorn make a delicious, immune-supporting fruit tea. It is best heated in a pan as a decoction; allow the berries to sit on a low heat for 20 minutes. The tea can also be used as a fruity, autumnal flavouring in cocktails.

Vinegars: Elderberries make delicious sharp drinking vinegars. Blend elderberry juice with apple cider vinegar and sugar to make a sweetly sharp vinegar to serve diluted with sparkling water or apple juice.

Juice: Heating ripe elderberries in a steamer or in a pan with a splash of water will release the juices and destroy any toxicity. Press the cooked berries through a sieve and freeze the juice in little pots to add to drinks through the year. The sieved pulp can be dehydrated and used like currants in baking.

Spiced elderberry port

Elderberries infused into port with a gentle hint of spices create a wonderfully warming tipple for cold winter evenings.

MAKES 850ML (1½ PINTS)
250g (9oz) ripe, destalked elderberries
½ cinnamon stick
2 cloves
1 star anise
500ml (18fl oz) tawny or ruby port
150ml (¼ pint) brandy
Demerara sugar (optional)

Place the elderberries in a saucepan with a splash of water. Place on a low heat and warm until the elderberries are soft. Pass the berries and juice through a sieve into a little saucepan (a milk pan is ideal), pressing to release the juice. Add the cinnamon, cloves and star anise to the pan and heat the juice until it comes to a simmer. Take the pan off the heat and leave to infuse for 1 hour.

Strain out the spices and pour the elderberry juice – there should be 200ml (7fl oz) – into a sterilized 1 litre (1¾ pint) bottle with the port and brandy. Leave for 2 weeks for the flavours to blend before tasting. If you would like to add sweetness, stir in some demerara sugar, a heaped teaspoon at a time, tasting after each spoonful is added.

This is best drunk straight away, but it will keep for up to 3 months. Once opened, store in the fridge and use within 3–4 weeks.

Elderberry, elderflower & honeysuckle cordial

Until recently, elder and honeysuckle were botanical family members, but they were sadly split up – a shame because they are so good together in this syrup of flowers and berries. This can be made with either homemade or shop-bought cordial (no one needs to know).

MAKES 600ML (1 PINT)
200g (7oz) ripe, destalked elderberries
500ml (18fl oz) elderflower cordial (see page 69)
Handful of honeysuckle flowers
   (green ends removed)

Place the berries in a saucepan with a splash of the cordial and heat until the berries become squishy. Press them with a masher, then strain through a sieve into a saucepan, pressing to extract the juice (keep the berries to add to apple crumbles).

Add the remaining cordial and the honeysuckle flowers to the juice in the pan and leave to infuse for a few hours. Strain the cordial back into the pan and bring it to a simmer. Transfer to sterilized bottles and store in the fridge for up to a month.

Hops
Humulus lupulus

If you are reading this book with a glass of beer in your hand, the bitter flavour of your drink comes from the plant you're reading about right now, hops. Perfectly ripe, aromatic hop flowers are harvested each summer and autumn – hop farms look like high rope courses, with thousands of the plants climbing networks of ropes that head skywards. These plants are not only skilled at growing upwards, they're also adept at spreading outwards, escaping and finding their way into hedgerows and up telegraph poles.

If you come across a hop bine growing wild, keep checking it until the flowers are ripe. Look inside them and you'll find a yellow waxy substance called lupulin, which is where the flavour of beer comes from. Not only a bitter flavouring and preservative, it is also traditionally used to aid relaxation, promote sleep and reduce anxiety (even without the addition of alcohol). Hops are a versatile ingredient in other drinks too. Alongside their bitter flavour, perfectly ripe hops have a sweet, fruity flavour that turns into wonderful syrups, soft drinks, cocktails and mocktails.

Edible parts: Young shoots (gathered in the spring) and flowers.

Harvesting: When hop flowers mature in summer or early autumn, they need to be harvested quickly because as they turn brown their flavour changes from fruity and sweet to garlicky. Gather them when the cone-like flowers have opened and feel papery. Mature hops will turn a pale green. Use fresh hops within 48 hours, ideally sooner, or dry them in a dehydrator on its lowest setting until they are brittle. The lupulin is affected by oxygen so storing hops in a vacuum bag helps retain their flavour (some people store them in the freezer).

Pairs with: Elderflower, grapefruit, apple, lemon, orange, rosehip, dried fruit, cream and custard.

Locations: Hedgerows, sign posts, telegraph poles and trees – often found in commercial hop-growing areas.

Caution: Take care using hops if you have an oestrogen-related condition. Hops are poisonous to dogs and should be kept away from where they could access them. When gathering hop shoots, take care to correctly identify the plant. There are a number of inedible climbing plants that look like hops in the spring.

How to drink: hops

Hops' reputation for bitterness dismisses the many other flavours in the flower – fruit, citrus and floral. These flavours are the first to be extracted, before the bitter notes come out. If you want to capture less of the bitterness, infuse the flower swiftly – you might find a few minutes is enough. Be aware that each hop will have a different strength of flavour so keep tasting your drinks as you infuse them.

 Beer: Most beer is made from dried hops. But for a couple of weeks each year, brewers head to the bines and harvest fresh hops to turn immediately into green hop beer – a light, delicious seasonal brew.

 Tea: Hop flowers are widely used to promote sleep and reduce anxiety. Serve hot, or chilled as an iced tea, either alone or with herbs such as lemon balm, lavender or linden flowers.

 Liqueurs: Hop liqueurs are made by steeping the flowers with sugar and lemon zest in a neutral spirit. To make a light-tasting drink, leave to infuse for a short time; for a strong bitter liqueur, infuse for a few days. Many amaros use hops in their herbal blends.

 Bitters/tinctures: Pack hop flowers into a jar, cover with a neutral spirit and leave to macerate for a few weeks before straining. Adding citrus peel such as grapefruit makes delicious bitters.

 Cordials/syrups: Infuse fresh or dried hops into sugar syrups with a squeeze of citrus. Hop-infused syrup can be enjoyed in cocktails or with sparkling water.

The hop orchard

When hops are at perfect ripeness, they have an apple flavour, reflecting the fruit that comes into harvest at the same time. And just as they grow together, so they go together, creating a drink of the early autumn filled with the perfume of hops and ripe apples. This drink is also delicious as a non-alcoholic cocktail, just leave the hops to infuse in the apple juice for longer if you don't use vodka.

SERVES 2
100ml (3½fl oz) vodka
400ml (14fl oz) apple juice
2 hop flowers
Ice cubes
A piece of grapefruit zest

Pour the vodka and apple juice into a jug, add the hop flowers and leave to infuse for 2 minutes.

Fill two glasses with ice and pour over the infused drink. Push the hop flowers into the drinks if you like bitter flavours, or discard if you're more sweetly inclined. Take the piece of grapefruit zest and squeeze it (skin on the outside) over the drinks so that the grapefruit oils drop in; rub the rims of the glasses with the zest and enjoy.

Hop, elderflower & lemon zest for life tea

Like hops, elderflowers and lemons have both been traditionally used to help alleviate symptoms of stress and, just as they work together herbally, so they also blend incredibly well as flavours. If you've ever had an elderflower- or citrus-flavoured beer you'll know how well. This blend can be drunk as a soothing hot tea or as a chilled drink served over ice.

FILLS A 150ML (5FL OZ) JAR
Dried peel of 1 lemon, finely chopped
30g (1oz) dried elderflowers
10g (¼ oz) dried hops, pulled apart

Place the peel, flowers and hops in a bowl and stir until well combined; spoon into a jar and store for up to 12 months.

To make the tea, use ½ teaspoon per person and infuse in just-boiled water for 5 minutes before drinking. You can also turn this blend into a syrup by soaking the ingredients in a hot sugar syrup for 2 hours.

Hazel
Corylus spp.

When you think of hazelnuts and drinks, you might imagine the syrupy nut-flavoured coffees drunk in their millions every day, often containing no real hazelnut, just artificial flavourings and even more sugar. Yet hazelnut coffee's origins come from a far less ultra-processed place. Legend has it that Alpine monks added ground hazelnuts to their coffee to help them stay alert during long nights of prayer. Adding nuts didn't just boost the flavour of the coffee, but also provided a nutritional boost because hazelnuts are crammed full of health benefits – omega fatty acids, B vitamins, copper, manganese and even heart-supporting folates. A million miles away from modern takeaway drinks.

Hazelnuts are also known as filberts, which means 'full beard' – a name that came from the beardy papery cups the nuts grow in. By early autumn, the ripe nuts start falling from the trees and in no time the shells are emptied by squirrels and mice. To beat the competition, you might need to harvest them before they fall. Gather as soon as the nuts fill their shells – they will be milky and fresh, a seasonal treat. Should you only have a few nuts in your harvest, you can turn them into the most delicious liqueur, which probably tastes even better knowing that no matter how many nuts the squirrels eat, they'll never enjoy them in such a delicious way.

Edible parts: Catkins, leaves and nuts.

Harvesting: The catkins appear in late winter, followed by the leaves in early spring. There are many different species of hazelnut, with nuts ripening from late summer to mid autumn. Crack open a nut to check that they are ready to harvest before picking the rest.

Pairs with: Chocolate, coffee, cream, vanilla, sweet woodruff, cinnamon, fig leaf, evergreens.

Locations: Hazels are often planted in hedgerows; traditionally coppiced, they often grow as multi-stemmed trees.

How to drink: hazel

Hazel drinking starts from late winter with the catkins, which are rich in proteins and minerals and decorate the tree. They are powdery, astringent and bitter. The leaves are milder, but the sweetest part of the tree is found in the nuts. Milky and slightly astringent when fresh, they can be roasted to bring out a sweeter flavour. Toast the shelled nuts in a heavy frying pan over a gentle heat or spread out on a baking tray and place in the oven at 180°C (350°F), Gas Mark 4, for 10 minutes. Place them in a tea towel and rub away the bitter skins before using.

Liqueurs: Hazelnuts make delicious syrupy liqueurs, the most famous of which is Frangelico – made with toasted nuts, infused with additional flavours of cacao bean, coffee, vanilla, orange blossom, fruit and roots.

Coffee: Findikli kahve is a Turkish coffee made by blending ground hazelnuts with coffee beans. You can make your own by brewing 1 spoonful of ground hazelnuts with 2 spoonfuls of ground Arabica coffee.

Cordials/syrups: Make true hazelnut syrup by infusing toasted chopped hazelnuts into sugar syrup.

Milks: Soak 1 cup of hazelnuts in water overnight before rinsing and blending with 2 cups of water, a pinch of salt, and maple syrup or vanilla to sweeten. Hazelnut milk can be fermented with kefir grains to make a plant probiotic drink.

Tea: Hazel leaves and catkins can be drunk as teas, considered traditionally to have astringent and blood-purifying qualities. Hazel catkins and leaves can be brewed alone, or mixed with black tea, giving the drink a mellow, almost chocolatey taste.

Fermented drinks: Adding hazelnuts to mead gives the drink a creamy, gently nutty taste.

Hazelnut syrup

True hazelnut syrup is less strongly flavoured than commercial syrups but is far nicer and with the added bonus of sweet, sticky hazelnut pieces to add to cakes and puddings. Use the syrup in cocktails and, of course, coffees.

_____

MAKES 250ML (9FL OZ)
250g (9oz) hazelnuts, chopped
250g (9oz) sugar
250ml (9fl oz) water

Toast the chopped hazelnuts in a heavy-based frying pan on a medium heat until they turn light brown and release a toasted, nutty aroma.

Place the toasted nuts in a saucepan with the sugar and water and heat, stirring, until the sugar has dissolved. Bring to the boil, turn the heat to the lowest setting and simmer for 10 minutes.

Remove from the heat and allow the nuts to steep for at least 2 hours (or overnight for a stronger flavour). Strain into a sterilized bottle and store in the fridge for up to 2 weeks.

Hazelnut liqueur

Hazelnuts make the most delicious liquor – you can use roasted nuts to get a warm flavour but, when in season, freshly shelled hazelnuts have a unique milky flavour that turns into a sensational liqueur. If you only have access to dried nuts, toast them first. Hazelnut liqueur is lovely by itself but you can also add additional flavours such as cocoa, coffee or spices like vanilla to it.

_____

MAKES 450ML (16FL OZ)
300g (10oz) freshly shelled hazelnuts
450ml (16fl oz) neutral spirit such as vodka
50g (2oz) sugar

Finely chop the hazelnuts to increase their surface area. Place the nuts in a wide-necked jar and add the alcohol and sugar. Steep for at least 6 weeks, shaking the jar each day, until you are happy with the flavour.

Strain the liqueur and add the boozy nuts to puddings and chocolate truffles.

Wild plum
Prunus spp.

Unless you live in Antarctica, you will have a type of plum growing near you. There are hundreds of different varieties, with fruit that ranges from purple to red, yellow and green, sour to sweet, and some almost bitterly astringent. They are all edible, but you need to make sure you have a plum. Growing as small trees with trunks that, over time, gain horizontal splits in the bark, all plums have small clusters of spring-opening flowers with five rounded petals and oval or rounded fruit with a join running from the top to the bottom. The flesh can be red or yellow-green and in the middle is a single, flat stone. Each species has a different-shaped or patterned stone, used to work out the variety of plum tree, just like a fingerprint.

You don't need to be an expert to turn plums into delicious drinks. Just let their taste be your guide. Lip-puckeringly sour fruits are best made into syrups or preserved like Chinese sour plums, which are fermented into salty umeboshi used across South Asia in everything from teas, sodas and sake-based liqueurs. Damsons (illustrated), on the other hand, have jammy rich flavours and produce incredible sour, fruity juices that make bright pink and vibrantly flavoured cordials and cocktails. Just remember, if you've got a good plum, you've got a good drink ahead of you.

Edible parts: Flowers, leaves and fruit.

Harvesting: Plums are best harvested when still slightly firm as they will ripen in the kitchen. Lay them out in a single layer until you want to use them to prevent any mould from damaged plums spreading.

Pairs with: Cinnamon, vanilla, cardamom, star anise, fennel, thyme, rum, amaretto, brandy, vodka and gin.

Locations: Plums grow in a wide range of habitats, from coastlines to urban streets. Plums thrive best in full sun, so look out for trees that aren't shaded for the best harvests.

How to drink: wild plum

Young leaves and plum blossoms can be infused into wines, liqueurs, syrups, teas and fermented drinks. Use them fresh or dried.

Wine: Plums make delicious full-bodied fruit wines. The yeasts and the tannins in the skins make them an excellent fruit to start making wine.

Liqueurs: These can be made with a wide range of base alcohols. Plum blossoms and young leaves can be infused in wines and brandy to make almond-flavoured aperitifs. In Japan, fermented plums are added to sake to make a liqueur. It is typically made with unripe fermented plums known as umeboshi, but you can also buy sake infused with ripe plums (known as nakata aka umeshu). In England, fermented plum juice is sometimes added to cider, creating a drink known as jerkum.

Cordials/syrups: Plum cordials can be cooling in hot weather, but can also be enjoyed through the winter months. Add spices such as cinnamon, clove, ginger and star anise to a winter cordial; try adding cooling flavours like rose or honeysuckle to summer cordials.

Tea: Plums are a valued ingredient in traditional remedies and are added to teas in Chinese and Ayurvedic medicines. Dry plums to add to tea blends.

Fermented drinks: The wild yeasts contained in the powdery dusting on the skin, the large amount of tannins and the sugar content make plums ideal for fermenting. Within a few days of juicing they will start to ferment. The juice can be diluted to make wild sodas. Add slices of plum to the second stage of fermentation when making kombucha and kefir.

Vinegars: Plums make delicious drinking vinegars by steeping the fruit in sweetened apple cider vinegar for a few weeks, or homemade plum vinegar.

Juice: Extract by using a juicer or gently cooking the plums in a pan with water. In India, plum juice is often used to make cold drinks, with the addition of spices including cumin and pepper.

Fermented plum brandy

In this traditional Transylvanian drink, plums are fermented in brown sugar, then the syrupy juices are added to brandy, making a fruity liqueur.

————

MAKES 1 LITRE (1³/₄ PINTS)
1kg (2lb 4oz) plums
400g (14oz) demerara sugar
About 500ml (18fl oz) brandy

Cut the plums in half, remove the stones and place in a sterilized wide-necked jar. Sprinkle over the sugar, coating the plums, then cover and leave for 2 hours. Mash the plums to release their juices, then pour over enough water to just cover them. Seal the jar and leave to ferment for 2 weeks, stirring every couple of days.

Pour the plums and liquid through a fine sieve and collect the fermented juice in a measuring jug. Add the same quantity of brandy as there is juice, mix together and pour into a sterilized bottle. Keep in the fridge and drink within a month.

Plum pudding liqueur

Quite literally a pudding and a liqueur – you can turn the cooked plums into a boozy fruit base for an autumnal crumble, making this well worth making again (and again).

————

MAKES 500ML (18FL OZ)
1kg (2lb 4oz) plums, halved and stoned
125ml (4fl oz) water
150ml (5fl oz) amaretto
About 250ml (9fl oz) spiced rum

Place the plums in a wide saucepan with a well-fitting lid, add the water, cover and place on a low heat to cook the plums. When the plums are soft, turn off the heat and pour in the amaretto. Leave to infuse for 10 minutes before straining through a sieve.

Reserve the soaked fruit for a pudding, then pour the liquid into a sterilized bottle and add the same volume of rum to plum liquid.

Drink neat as a liqueur (perhaps served with a crumble made from the soaked plums), or make into a Plum pudding cocktail: place 4 tablespoons of the liqueur into a cocktail shaker, add ¹/₂ teaspoon of dried meadowsweet (optional) and 4 tablespoons of sour apple juice. Shake and serve over ice.

Hawthorn
Crataegus spp.

Hawthorns are small trees historically used as a hedging plants providing stock proofing for early enclosed fields. But hawthorns aren't only found in hedgerows; the small, gnarly trunked trees crop up in fields, wasteland and on mountainsides. In the early spring they are among the earliest trees to turn green with new foliage – hard to miss with their young, lobed leaves in vibrant green. These leaves make a fresh addition to springtime teas and fortified wine liqueurs.

Just weeks after their leaves open, their flowers bloom – little creamy white five-petalled flowers that cover the tree with blossom and fill the air with a heady scent. Hawthorn's final display comes in the early autumn when clusters of red fruits, like small apples, decorate the trees. If you open up the berry, you might find that it has one or two seeds and, in the case of Chinese hawthorn (*Crataegus pinnatifida*), seeds that look like apple pips. This is no accident, as hawthorn trees are part of the same family of plants as apples and share distinctly apple-like flavours, especially Chinese hawthorn, which you'll find throughout the winter in China being sold on sticks, covered in hard candy just like toffee apples.

Edible parts: Leaves, flowers and berries.

Harvesting: In the spring, collect the tender freshly opened leaves. Late spring brings the blossoms – some species of hawthorn have a less appealing scent than others; leave these on the tree as their scent transfers into flavour in the form of berries. Harvest ripe berries through autumn until early winter.

Pairs with: Leaves with nettle, flowering currant and lemon balm; flowers with vanilla, honey, ginger, orange, sloe, nettle and apple.

Locations: Hedgerows, scrubland, fields and hillsides.

Caution: Avoid hawthorn if on heart medication.

How to drink: hawthorn

Hawthorn leaves provide a tonic in the spring, the flowers give floral flavours in early summer and the vitamin C-rich berries a warming boost when needed in the autumn. Hawthorn berries are quite dry, but if soaked overnight in hot water, they will release their flavour into the liquid. Hawthorn juice is drunk as a tonic in China where it is mixed with other fruits, including strawberry juice.

 Wine: Hawthorn berries make a fruity, dry wine. Add citric acid or oranges, and pectinase to prevent the wine from becoming cloudy.

 Tea: The leaves, flowers and berries can all be drunk as tea – dried berries are best used in a decoction-style drink.

 Liqueurs: The leaves, flowers and berries all make delicious liqueurs. Infuse young hawthorn leaves in brandy and sugar to make an almond-flavoured drink. The flowers can be added to vodka with apple juice, while the berries can be steeped in brandy or gin – adding hawthorn berries to sloe gin gives a warming flavour.

 Fermented drinks: Adding hawthorn berries to second stage kombucha fermentation brings out the fruit's apple-like flavours.

 Vinegars: Hawthorn vinegar is a refreshing immune-boosting tonic. Hawthorn berries make a sweet, fruity drinking vinegar; either add as a flavouring to live cider vinegar or use a starter to make your own. Enjoy sweetened with honey and diluted with water.

 Cordials/syrups: Hawthorn flowers and berries make great-tasting cordials and syrups. Simmer the berries in a pan of apple juice, using one part berries to three parts juice. Strain and reheat with sugar or honey before bottling.

Warming mulled hawthorn berry & apple

Warming spices with hawthorn and apples make a beautiful mulled drink. If you want to make a more adult drink, add a serving of Hawthorn & Orange Brandy (see right) to make a hot toddy.

_____

SERVES 6–8

1kg (2lb 4oz) mixed hawthorn berries and apples
½ teaspoon salt
1 cinnamon stick
2 cloves
5 allspice berries
1.5 litres (2¾ pints) boiling water
100g (3½oz) granulated sugar or light honey

Rinse the hawthorn berries several times in fresh water, then place in a bowl with the salt. Cover the berries with water and leave to soak for 10 minutes before rinsing. Meanwhile, grate the apples.

Place the berries in a large bowl and use a potato masher to squash them until the skins split open. Add the grated apples and spices and cover with the just-boiled water. Cover and leave for 24 hours to infuse.

Pass the liquid through a fine sieve into a saucepan and heat gently. Sweeten with sugar or honey before serving.

Hawthorn & orange brandy

This makes a warming tipple for winter evenings. You can leave the berries to infuse for longer than two weeks, but be aware that the large amount of pectin in the fruit will start to dissolve into the liqueur, making it cloudy. If that happens, don't despair. Your drink will still be delicious, just less beautiful.

_____

MAKES 1 LITRE (1¾ PINTS)

200g (7oz) hawthorn berries
Pared zest of 2 organic oranges
100g (3½oz) unrefined light brown sugar
1 litre (1¾ pints) brandy

Place the berries in a large jar with the zest and sugar before pouring over the brandy. Shake the jar each day for 2 weeks before straining out the berries and zest. Drink within a few weeks of opening.

Oak
Quercus spp.

Oak trees thrive everywhere from dense woodland and salty coastlines to arid, baking savannas. Only more diverse than their habitats are the wide range of species in their clan – there are hundreds of different oak trees, divided into two groups: red oaks and white oaks. There are two key ways to work out what group your tree falls into: firstly, white oaks have rounded lobed leaves, while those of the red oak are pointed. Secondly, if you look at the cup of the acorn, white oaks have a smaller cup, while red oaks have larger ones (bigger than the acorn).

Both white and red oaks have significant amounts of tannins in their leaves, and even more in their nuts (acorns) making them astringent and unpleasant to eat raw. While there are fewer tannins in acorns from white oaks, acorns from both types of tree need to be soaked to extract the tannins to make them edible. Fortunately, tannins are water soluble so you can leach them out of acorns by chopping and soaking them in a number of changes of cold water. This can take a few days, depending on the amount of tannins. Once the tannins have been dissolved into the water, the acorns become sweet and nutty – perfect for making liqueurs to sip in ancient woodlands or even hot savannas.

Edible parts: Leaves, acorns, twigs and bark.

Harvesting: Collect twigs with swelling leaf buds in the spring before they start to open. Harvest the young, tender leaves for a couple of weeks after they open. Collect acorns in autumn, discarding any that are blackened or have holes in the shells. Dried leaves can be collected through late autumn and into winter.

Pairs with: Spring leaves with lemon, orange and pine; acorns with spices, roots, brandy, vodka, sloe, rosehip and hawthorn.

Locations: Woodland and open spaces in a wide range of climates and altitudes.

Caution: Even if your acorns don't taste astringent, they will need soaking in water before using.

How to drink: oak

Oak trees provide flavours throughout the year, from fresh, acidic young leaves to woody twigs and sweet acorns. Some years, oak trees will produce huge harvests of acorns, others very little, so in an abundant year, harvest enough to dry acorns and store them in case the following year's pickings are lean.

Wine: Both young green leaves in spring and older brown autumn leaves can be used to make oak leaf wine – the spring wine tastes light and fresh, the autumn wine is sweeter and warming.

Fermented drinks: Oak leaves can be added to kombucha at the first fermentation stage. Recent research indicates that oak leaves in kombucha increase its anti-inflammatory abilities.

Beer: Some craft beermakers use young oak leaves to make beer with a barrel-aged taste.

Bitters/tinctures: Acorns, twigs and bark are used in bitters to add smoky, woody flavours.

Liqueurs: Roasted acorns are used to make a delicious Spanish sweet liqueur (see right).

Coffee: Leached and roasted acorns can be ground into a coffee with a nutty, charred chocolate flavour. Acorn coffee can be blended with cleavers seeds and dandelion, chicory and burdock root to make a wild coffee infusion.

Acorn liqueur (licor de bellota)

This golden, nutty, sweet liqueur is made in southwest Spain, tasting almost of praline. It is delicious served over ice, with sparkling wine or as the sweet element in an autumnal cocktail with sloe gin.

MAKES 1.2 LITRES (2 PINTS)
200g (7oz) acorns, roughly chopped and leached
150g (5oz) golden sugar
400ml (14fl oz) water
700ml (1¼ pints) brandy or vodka

Preheat the oven to 175°C (350°F), Gas Mark 6. Spread out the leached acorns on a baking tray and roast for 10–20 minutes or until the acorns are dark brown.

Meanwhile, place the sugar and water in a large saucepan and bring to the boil, stirring until the sugar has dissolved. Add the roasted acorns to the sugary water, then leave to cool. Pour the acorns and liquid into a large jar, add the brandy, seal and place in a dark cupboard for up to 8 weeks (but you can drink it before then if you're impatient for a splash of acorn in your drink).

Pass the liqueur through a fine sieve into a sterilized bottle and enjoy within a year.

Oak leaf wine

You can make this wine with very young, freshly opened oak leaves or, at the other end of the season, with brown leaves (only harvest brown leaves that are still on the tree). Both have distinctive flavours that capture the season. If you use the older leaves, replace the lemon with another orange.

MAKES 6 X 700ML (1¼ PINT) BOTTLES
1kg (2lb 4oz) sugar
4.6 litres (8 pints) water
400g (14oz) oak leaves
225g (8oz) sultanas, washed and chopped
Juice of 1 orange
Juice of 1 lemon
¼ teaspoon malt extract
10g (¼oz) wine yeast

Place the sugar and water in a large saucepan and heat, stirring, until the sugar has dissolved, then remove from the heat and leave to cool.

Wash the oak leaves and place into a sterilized container with the sultanas, orange and lemon juice and the malt extract. Pour the sweetened cooled water over the leaf mixture and leave to soak for 24 hours.

Strain the liquid from the leaves and pour into a sterilized fermenting container. Add the yeast, cover and leave for 3 days until bubbles start appearing.

Pour the liquid into a sterilized demijohn with an airlock and allow the wine to ferment before racking and bottling (see page 239). It will be ready to drink after a few months of racking.

Sea buckthorn
Hippophae spp.

Like gorse, sea buckthorn is a spiny coast-loving shrub that forms dense thickets around cool northern coastlines and mountains. While gorse's leaves are spiny and hard, the foliage of sea buckthorn is silvery and soft, looking like a cross between willow and olive. However, it hides sharp thorns growing from its branches.

In the autumn and winter, sea buckthorn shrubs turn bright orange as they are covered with little berries crammed full of sour juices. Imagine a tangy passion fruit mixed with an unripe mango and you'll be close to the wincingly sour but incredible taste of a sea buckthorn berry. Sea buckthorn has a long and revered reputation as a superfood – in Nepal, it's known as the Gold Lucky Tree, while others know it as the Miracle Fruit. And quite rightly so – sea buckthorn berries are among the most nutrient-dense foods in the world, rich in omega-3, -6, -7 and -9 oils, fibre, folic acid, iron, micronutrients and vast amounts of vitamin C. Even the leaves are rich in antioxidants, amino acids and fatty acids. No wonder every year foragers battle the thorns to collect their sea buckthorn prize.

Edible parts: Berries and leaves.

Harvesting: The ripe berries are very soft and juicy. Either harvest them directly into a container, or gather them by the stem and freeze the whole stem before you pull the frozen berries into a tub. This prevents you from getting covered in juices. The leaves can be harvested in spring to autumn, the berries in autumn to winter.

Pairs with: Rosehip, passion fruit, mango, apricot, pear, ginger, rosemary, juniper, rum, gin and vodka.

Locations: Mainly found on the coasts of Europe and mountains of Asia, sea buckthorn has been introduced to North America as a crop and is now spreading across the states. Look for it on sandy dunes, often growing right up to the shoreline.

Caution: Take care to avoid the spiny thorns when harvesting from sea buckthorn.

How to drink: sea buckthorn

Extract the juice from sea buckthorn berries by pressing them through a sieve. If you store your juice for any time you might notice that it splits, with a clearer liquid at the top – these are the fat-rich oils. Simply shake the bottle before you use it. Sea buckthorn juice can be stored in the fridge for up to a month or in ice cube trays to add to drinks later in the year.

 Beer: Sea buckthorn's tart, citrusy flavours are put to good use by craft brewers who add them to their brews to make sour saison-style drinks.

 Tea: Both the leaves and berries can be used to make teas that are especially beneficial if you are run down. Try blending the leaves and berries with rosemary and ginger and sweetening with honey.

 Liqueurs: Across Europe, sea buckthorn berries are infused into liqueurs. Either soak the whole berries to keep a clear liqueur or mash them for a bright orange drink. Sweeten with honey or sugar.

 Fermented drinks: While sea buckthorn is already a superfood, fermenting the berry is said to increase its ample benefits. Try adding the berries to kombucha, tepache or ginger beer.

 Cordials/syrups: Paired with vanilla, sea buckthorn berries make a delicious cordial sweetened with honey or sugar – use in soft drinks or in cocktails.

Sea buckthorn & apricot mule

Sea buckthorn, ginger and apricot is a great flavour pairing (or trio-ing), especially in Moscow Mule-style drinks. The sweetness of the jam counteracts the tang of the sea buckthorn and ginger beer. This is delicious whether served in a copper jug or not.

SERVES 2
120ml (4fl oz) vodka
2 tablespoons sea buckthorn juice
2 teaspoons apricot jam
Ice cubes
200ml (7fl oz) good-quality ginger beer

Divide the vodka and sea buckthorn juice between two glasses and spoon in the jam. Stir until the jam has dissolved. Add a few cubes of ice before topping with the ginger beer.

Tepache with sea buckthorn

Tepache is a Mexican fermented drink, making use of the flesh and yeast-covered skins of ripe pineapples – ideal for using up pineapple that's languishing in your fruit bowl. Recent research has discovered that, as with lots of plants, fermenting sea buckthorn supercharges its nutritional benefits.

MAKES ABOUT 1 LITRE (1³/₄ PINTS)
1 extremely ripe pineapple
180g (6¹/₄oz)unrefined sugar
15g (¹/₂oz) fresh ginger
1 litre (1³/₄ pints) water
4 tablespoons sea buckthorn berries (smashed),
    or juice (2 tablespoons if you're using
    powdered berries)

Lightly rinse and slice the pineapple into large chunks (you want the yeasts on the skins as this is what starts the fermentation). Place the sugar, grated ginger and a cup of the water in a 2 litre (3¹/₂ pint) jar and stir to start dissolving the sugar.

Push the pineapple chunks into the jar and fill with the rest of the water, making sure the pineapple is completely covered. Cover with a piece of cloth and ferment at room temperature for 3 days (stirring occasionally).

Once the liquid starts bubbling, stir in the sea buckthorn, leave for another day before straining and bottling in strong bottles with flip-top lids. After a couple of days, the drink will have become carbonated and is ready to drink. Serve ice cold with a sprig of rosemary.

Crab apple
Malus sylvestris

While cultivated apples are bred for sweetness, size and bite, crab apples can be incredibly sour and tannic. Crab apples are wild apples, so-called because of their small size and sour flavour. They are often overlooked as a food source – if you've bitten into one raw, you'll probably understand why. But the sourness makes them a wild drink maker's friend. Cook them – peel, cores and all – in water and you'll extract the delicious sour juice to use in place of citrus juices. This liquid is not only deliciously sour, but is also full of pectin, which makes it thick and viscous.

Species of crab apple are often grown as ornamental specimens. While native European crab apples produce gnarly yellow fruit up to 5cm (2in) across, ornamental crab apples tend to be a lot smaller, ranging from tiny yellowy, orange or red round fruit no more than 2cm (¾in) across, to oblong fruit that look like rosehips. Fortunately, wild or ornamental, all crab apples (and their grapefruit-tasting blossom) are edible and, should you find a sour, tart variety, extremely drinkable.

Edible parts: Fruit, leaves and flowers.

Harvesting: Most crab apples look obviously like apples, but some look like a hard cherry or large rosehip. If you're not sure, slice the fruit in half and if the centre of the fruit has a star-shaped seed casing with one or two seeds in each section, you've got a crab apple. If your apple is sour, tangy, fruity and tannic (astringent), you've got a harvest worth gathering. If it's insipid, bland or even bitter, leave it. Look out for bloom in mid spring, crab apples in early autumn to late winter, and leaves from spring to autumn.

Pairs with: Rosehip, hawthorn, damson, elderberry, blackberry, sloe, elderflower, yarrow, mint, evergreens, cinnamon, vanilla, sweet woodruff, fennel, star anise, brandy, vodka, gin and whisky.

Locations: Wild crab apples are often found in hedgerows, woodland edges and scrubland. You will also often find them in gardens growing as ornamental trees.

How to drink: crab apple

In the spring, the newly opened blossom tastes like a combination of grapefruit, rose and almond. The leaves are astringent and rich in antioxidants, anti-inflammatories, and polyphenols and the crab apples create a sharp, fruity juice.

Liqueurs: Crab apples are a versatile ingredient in a wide range of spirits, from whisky and brandy to vodka and gin. Cut them in half and place in a jar with your chosen spirit and any spices you like. Make sure they are kept under the surface and soak for a few weeks. Sweeten once strained (crab apple syrup is a great sweetener). The blossoms can also be infused into spirits – soak them for an hour to extract their flavour before straining.

Cordials/syrups: Both the blossoms and fruit can be made into syrups. To make a blossom syrup, make a sugar syrup and pour it hot over the blossoms with a twist of grapefruit peel. Allow to steep for a few hours before straining. The sour liquid extracted by boiling whole crab apples in water can be turned into a lovely sharp syrup. Strain the pulp and pour the liquid into a pan with the same amount of sugar. Place on a gentle heat until the sugar has completely dissolved, then simmer for five minutes before bottling.

Thickeners: Crab apples contain a significant amount of pectin, a substance that provides thickness to drinks. The pectin is found mostly in the peel and cores, so cook whole apples in water until they collapse. Use a masher to break them up completely and leave to soak for a few hours before straining through a muslin cloth. The liquid that drips out is sour and thick, and will foam when shaken, making the perfect thickener for sour cocktails.

Tea: The flowers, leaves and fruit are all lovely in tea. The blossoms are very delicately flavoured and are best made into tea with cleavers and primroses, using just-boiled water or a cold water overnight infusion. The apples can be used fresh or dried in teas – try blending dried crab apples with dried elderflowers or hawthorn.

Fermented drinks: Crab apples ferment into a pink cider, which looks deceptively sweet (see opposite).

Crab apple cider

If you leave your crab apples to mature on the tree, the tannins become mellow and the sugars intensify. Gather a basket of these apples to make a delicious pink-hued cider. This recipe is for those of us who might just have a basket of fruit and no cider-making equipment, although you will need a fermentation vessel, ideally a demijohn.

————

MAKES 4.5 LITRES (8 PINTS)
2kg (4lb 8oz) crab apples, mouldy parts cut away
4 litres (7 pints) sharp apple juice
  (without preservatives or sugars added)
1 Campden tablet, crumbled
1 sachet of Champagne or cider yeast,
  about 5g (⅛oz) (optional)

Place the apples in a pan, cover with water and cook until soft. Add the apple juice and leave to cool. Strain through a cloth into a demijohn; add the Campden tablet and cover. After 24 hours, add the yeast, if using, fit a sterilized airlock to the demijohn and place in a cool room.

After a couple of days, the liquid should start bubbling. If you haven't added yeast and it hasn't started bubbling after 3 days, add a pinch. Leave until it stops bubbling and a layer of sediment has formed at the base (this can take a month or two.

Siphon the cider into a second demijohn, making sure it's completely full (add water if it's not) and seal with a lid. Store in a cool place for a few months. The cider should now be sweetly dry and flat. Make it sparkling by transferring it to 500ml (18fl oz) bottles and funnelling a flat teaspoon of sugar into each. Cap the bottles and, within a few days, the cider will be sparkling. It will keep for up to 2 years in the unopened bottles.

Lambswool wassail

Wassails are a British tradition that involves wishing bountiful harvests for your apple trees during the coming year. Traditionally, toasts are made with a wassail punch including this one known as a Lambswool, so named because of the fluffy apples that are stirred into it. (Omit the eggs if preferred.)

————

SERVES 6
500g (1lb 2oz) crab apples
1 litre (1¾ pints) cider or apple juice
250ml (9fl oz) brandy (optional)
150g (5oz) light brown sugar
2 cinnamon sticks
10 cloves
10 allspice berries
1 blade of mace
¼ nutmeg, grated
1 teaspoon ground ginger
2 eggs, separated

Score a slit in each apple, place them in an ovenproof dish, add a splash of water and cover with a tight lid. Place in a preheated oven at 120°C (250°F), Gas Mark 1/2, until they are soft. Meanwhile, place the cider or apple juice and brandy in a saucepan with half the sugar, the cinnamon, cloves, allspice and mace. Heat gently.

Push the pulp out of the apple skins and pass it through a fine sieve to make a soft, fluffy mixture. Stir in the remaining sugar, the nutmeg and ground ginger. Whisk the egg whites and yolks in separate bowls until fluffy. Just before serving, stir the whisked egg whites and yolks together and, once blended, pour over a ladle of the hot cider. Gently fold the drink into the eggs, adding the apple flesh. Finish with a final grate of nutmeg and ladle into cups.

Rowan or mountain ash
Sorbus spp.

Rowan trees, often called mountain ashes, are easiest to identify in late summer when they are adorned with huge clusters of bright red berries. You'll find rowan trees in gardens, town streets, parks and, as its other name suggests, on mountainsides. These are small trees with slender grey trunks that, if cut back, will grow multiple trunks like a coppiced hazel. The leaves are divided like small ash leaves but, unlike ash, rowan leaves are toothed or serrated around the edges.

Rowan berries are crammed full of vitamin C, vitamin E, beta-carotene and potassium. Herbalists use them as a medicine, used for healing digestion, lungs and the liver. Easy to find and quick to harvest, the large clusters of berries mean you can fill a basket in minutes but, despite all of their attributes, rowan berries aren't as commonly eaten as other wild fruit. If you ate a raw berry (don't) you'd know why; they are incredibly bitter and astringent. The reason for their unappealing flavour when raw is sorbic acid, a compound that renders the raw fruit inedible. Freezing or cooking renders this compound harmless and also *slightly* sweetens the berries. Luckily, the bitter, astringent, fruity flavour is welcomed in drinks making and, with a bit of know-how, the berries can be turned into very tasty beverages.

Edible parts: Leaf and flower buds, flowers and berries.

Harvesting: Collect leaf and flower buds in early spring, flowers in late spring or early summer. Gather ripe berries when they start softening and become juicy. If the birds are stripping the berries before they are ripe, collect and freeze them.

Pairs with: Ginger, honey, crab apple, dessert apple, lemon, heather, redcurrant, apricot, blackcurrant leaves, grape, cinnamon, goji berry and pepper.

Locations: Town planting, parks and mountain sides.

Caution: Rowan flowers, buds and berries all need to be heated to make them safe to consume.

How to drink: rowan

Rowan flower and leaf buds have an exquisite marzipan flavour but they need to be heated to be made safe to eat, so infuse them in hot syrups before using. The berries also need heating (and ideally freezing) before consuming.

Wine: In Wales, rowan berries were traditionally made into a drink known as diodgriafel and they also make a delicious wine.

Beer: Add the berries to homemade beers as a bitter flavouring (like hops).

Liqueurs: Across Europe, the berries are collected after the first hard frosts and covered with alcohol to make liquors. You can use any high-grade alcohol but fruit-based schnapps, brandy or eau de vie are ideal as they marry up with rowan's fruit flavour.

Distilled drinks: If you have a still and a licence to make your own alcohol, take inspiration from the distillers of the Tyrol, who turn rowan berries into beloved fragrant brandy-style spirits.

Cordials/syrups: The berries make a cordial that can be paired with apples to balance their flavour (or lemon juice or citric acid can be used instead). Infuse the unopened flower buds into warm sugar syrup to make it taste of marzipan.

Tea: Add dried berries to winter decoction tea blends (or use them in place of orange peel in the Douglas fir, orange peel & rosemary decoction tea on page 213). The leaves and flowers all lend a sweet almond flavour to spring herbal teas (and can be dried for use later).

Vinegars: Infuse rowan berries into sweetened vinegars to make shrubs – try pairing them with apples or redcurrants for a balanced fruity flavour. Or, make your vinegar from scratch as the juice ferments into a lovely vinegar.

Bitters/tinctures: Rowan berries make a great bittering ingredient. Use rowan in place of orange peel in bitters recipes.

Rowan-infused eau de vie

Rowan makes perfectly lovely drinks with most spirits but especially with those made from fruits. This is not a sweet drink but perhaps the closest thing you'll get to your own bottle of distilled rowan liquor without making it yourself. Freezing, heating and drying may seem like a faff, but these processes will bring out the sweet flavours of the fruit and transfer them to the drink.

_____

MAKES 500ML (18FL OZ)
250g (9oz) ripe rowan berries
500ml (18fl oz) eau de vie or schnapps

First freeze the berries for 1 week, then place them in a saucepan with a splash of water and thaw them over a low heat. Allow the berries to break up and simmer for a few minutes, stirring all the time to stop them from burning.

Remove the berries from the heat and spread out on a sheet of baking paper on a baking tray. Place in a very low oven or dehydrator and dry out until the berries are like a fruit leather.

Rip the pieces of rowan fruit up and place them in a jar. Cover with the eau de vie and leave to steep for 3 days before straining. The flavours of the rowan will have been captured by the spirit. Search online for how much a rowan eau de vie costs and toast your money-saving skills.

Rowan berry shrub

Rowan is part of the Rosaceae (rose) family, which is also home to apples. The fruit pair together like cousins who get on so well they wish they were siblings.

_____

MAKES 500ML (18FL OZ)
100g (3½oz) ripe rowan berries
200g (7oz) granulated sugar or honey
250ml (9fl oz) apple cider vinegar

First freeze the berries for 1 week, then allow to thaw. Place all the ingredients in a large jar, seal well and give the contents a shake. Leave for 1 week to macerate (shaking the jar each day).

Strain the sweetened vinegar into a sterilized bottle. To serve, place 2 tablespoons of rowan berry shrub in a glass, fill with ice and top up with soda, seltzer or sparkling water.

Sloe
Prunus spinosa

Sloes are the fruit of the blackthorn bush. Their name means 'bluish plum', but once you taste a sloe you might think that it ought to include 'incredibly sour' as a prefix. They are indeed so astringent that they will draw any moisture from your mouth – so, well described in Italian as the fruit that *legano i denti* (ties your teeth). The astringency of sloes comes from the fact they are packed full of tannins, which, combined with their incredible sourness, might put you off entirely. However, they make utterly moreish drinks and every year across Europe billions of sloes are packed into jars with alcohol and sugar and are turned into sweet liqueurs.

The flavours are fruity and tannic, with a hint of almond that comes from the kernels, and are soaked into the drink during a long steep in the alcohol. The almond flavour in sloe liqueur is also found in blackthorn flowers and early leaves, which open at the start of spring and, like their later fruit, are equally delicious drinks ingredients. Blackthorn flowers are gorgeous infused into syrups and the tender leaves are used in France to make troussepinette, an almond-flavoured liqueur made by soaking the newly opened leaves in wine fortified with Cognac or brandy.

Edible parts: Leaves, flowers and berries.

Harvesting: Blackthorn flowers open before the leaves; collect them on a sunny day for the sweetest flavour. Young leaves and tender tips can be picked for a few weeks after opening until they become tough. Sloe berries start looking ripe at the end of the summer but try to wait until the fruit starts to become slightly soft. This gives a chance for the fruitier, sweeter flavours to develop.

Pairs with: Nettle, meadowsweet, star anise, juniper, coffee, fennel, blackberry, apple, liquorice, vanilla, cardamom, gin, vodka, grappa, schnapps, port and brandy.

Locations: Old hedgerows, woodlands and scrubland.

Caution: Be careful not to get jabbed by the very spiky thorns as you collect your sloes, which can cause a painful swelling reaction and sometimes infection.

How to drink: sloe

Tasting like incredibly sour, tannic plums, sloes go a long way in terms of flavour. Allowing the skins to burst open in long infusions or in the heat of a pan lets the anthocyanin and tannin-rich flavours of the berries be absorbed into drinks.

Wine: The acidity, tannins and flavours of sloes create a deep red, rich wine worthy of sitting on the best of dinner tables. Flavoured infused fortified wines are made by infusing blackthorn leaves in fortified red, white or rosé wine. Sloes themselves can be soaked in a blend of red wine and brandy to make a port-style drink.

Liqueurs: The most well-known way to drink sloe is as a liqueur. Ripe sloes are soaked for months in spirits, delicious simply flavoured with sloes or laced with herbs and spices too, such as star anise, vanilla or coffee.

Cocktails: Sloe verjus makes a great souring ingredient for cocktails. Cook sloes in twice as much water to fruit until mushy. Leave to infuse for a couple of hours before straining, and store in the fridge for up to two weeks.

Cordials/syrups: Infuse blackthorn flowers into warm sugar syrups. Make cordials using the sloes – if you only have a small harvest, pair them with peeled and chopped apples.

Tea: Blackthorn leaves, flowers and sloes are used in herbal teas. Dried sloes brewed as a decoction tea, paired with pine needles, provide a vitamin C boost.

Fermented drinks: Sloes are delicious added to kombuchas by themselves or along with other hedgerow fruits, including rosehips and hawthorn. Make a cordial (see opposite) and, for a festive drink, dilute it with equal amounts of water and bottle. Within days it will start to fizz.

Vinegars: Mix equal amounts of cider vinegar, honey and softened sloes in a jar and leave to infuse for a few days before straining. Dilute with still or sparkling water as a drinking vinegar.

Sloe cordial

Sloe cordial is delicious as a hot or cold drink. It makes a beautiful mulled drink with hot apple juice and spices such as star anise, cardamom, vanilla and cinnamon. Make double what you think you need, because sloe cordial can also be used as the sweetener for an incredibly fruity sloe gin.

MAKES 600ML (1 PINT)
500g (1lb 2oz) sloes
1 litre (1³/₄ pints) water
Juice of about 2 lemons
About 400g (14oz) sugar

Place the sloes and water in a saucepan over a medium heat, stirring frequently to make sure the fruit doesn't burn on the base of the pan. Simmer for 15 minutes. When soft, squash them with a potato masher to release as much juice as possible.

Pour the mixture into a jelly bag or sieve lined with muslin, and drip the juice into a measuring jug (don't be tempted to squeeze the bag). Measure the amount of liquid before returning it to the pan. For every 100ml (3½fl oz) of juice, add 1 tablespoon of lemon juice and 80g (3oz) of sugar.

Place the pan on a medium heat and bring to a simmer, stirring, for a few minutes until the sugar has dissolved and the liquid is glossy. Pour into freshly sterilized bottles and store for up to 1 month (or a year if pasteurized). The discarded fruit and stones can be added to alcohol to make liqueurs like sloe gin (see opposite).

Sloe gin

Most gins work well for this recipe but a good standard London dry, with its strong juniper flavour, is one of the best to use. This version of sloe gin is made in two stages: first, infusing the fruit and then adding sweetness, which will avoid creating an overly sweet drink, more like cough mixture.

MAKES 1 LITRE (1³/₄ PINTS)
1kg (2lb 4oz) sloes
750ml (1 pint 7fl oz) gin
500g (1lb 2oz) sugar
100ml (3½fl oz) water

If your sloes are not soft, place them in the freezer overnight to split their skins. Thaw them in a warm room as this will help open up the juices before adding them to the gin. Place the sloes in a wide-necked jar and cover with the gin. Leave the jar in a cupboard for 3 months.

Make a syrup by placing the sugar and water in a saucepan on a medium heat, stirring until the sugar has dissolved. Do not burn the syrup; it should be clear, not caramelized.

Drain the sloe-infused gin through a fine sieve into a bowl. Pour in half the syrup and taste; add more syrup according to your own preference. If you like sour drinks and your friends like them sweeter, serve sloe gin with a bottle of syrup or sloe cordial to allow them to sweeten their own. Transfer the liquid to a sterilized bottle and leave the syrup and gin to blend for a week before drinking (if you can).

Sweet chestnut
Castanea sativa

These trees, like their oak and beech relatives, grow large and are long lived; it's not unusual for chestnuts to live for 500 years and some live for thousands. The bark develops net-like patterns, creating a spiral as the aging trunk twists. Growing in an open spot, it may have low-hanging branches, making its large lance-shaped, toothed leaves easy to spot. Not only useful for identifying the tree, the leaves can also be harvested to make herbal teas famed for their antibacterial properties. In the summer, chestnut flowers grow like long creamy catkins.

Come autumn, it is time for the chestnuts to ripen and be turned into warming, nourishing food and drinks, the nutty smell of roasting chestnuts permeating the cold air. Rich in carbohydrates, minerals and vitamins, including B vitamins and vitamin C, these nuts are a source of immune-supporting antioxidants. This blend of nutrition, nutty flavour, starches and sweetness make them ideal candidates to sup in drinks as you roast even more on an open fire.

Edible parts: Leaves, flowers and nuts.

Harvesting: Chestnuts are best collected from the ground. Wear gardening gloves to handle them or press on the shells with your foot to release the nut from its spiky case.

Pairs with: Vanilla, pine, red wine, port, elderberry, coffee, pear, quince, honey, cinnamon, maple syrup, rum and orange.

Locations: Woodland, parkland and estates.

Caution: Take care not to confuse chestnuts with horse chestnuts (conkers). They have rounded leaves and more rubbery cases with fewer spikes that are softer than those of sweet chestnuts.

How to drink: chestnut

Don't despair if you haven't had a good sweet chestnut harvest – the edible non-nut parts of the tree are delicious in their own right. Even if you collect the chestnuts only to find their shells are empty, you can still use their woody exterior to make syrups and liqueurs.

 Wine: Portuguese winemakers soak chestnut flowers in white wine as it ferments to add a honeyed floral flavour. In Asia, the nuts are used in a chestnut rice wine known as makgeolli.

 Tea: Spring-harvested chestnut leaves and flowers can be made into fresh tea or dried to drink later in the year. Rich in tannins, chestnut leaf tea is often sweetened with honey.

 Beer: Chestnuts are a great ingredient for making gluten-free beer, used in place of the grains traditionally used in beermaking.

 Fermented drinks: The flowers are full of wild yeasts and ferment into sweetly sparkling wild sodas and champagnes. The flowers and nuts are both used in kombuchas.

 Liqueurs: The flowers and nuts make lovely liqueurs. Soak chopped nuts in vodka, rum or brandy for a month then sweeten with unrefined sugar or maple syrup (using raw or roasted nuts will give different flavours).

 Warming/milky drinks: Pair finely chopped roasted chestnuts with rooibos tea, and add spices like cinnamon, ginger and vanilla to make warming chai drinks.

 Cordials/syrups: Chestnut flowers, nuts and even the shells can infuse into syrups. If using the nuts, follow the recipe for Hazelnut syrup (on page 159). The shells give a woody flavour; soak them in boiled water first to make a tea that is then used to dissolve the sugar in. Add vanilla or cinnamon for a warming flavour.

 Milks: Purée chestnuts that have been soaked overnight in water, then strain the liquid through a muslin to make chestnut milk. The leftover pulp can be used in baking. Chestnut milk is lovely on its own or flavoured with cardamom, cinnamon or vanilla.

Imbuljuta tal-qastan

Imbuljuta tal-qastan is a warming, spiced Maltese drink enjoyed after midnight mass on Christmas and New Year's Eve. The chestnuts are traditionally left whole, giving a welcome snack to have with the drink.

————

SERVES 6
250g (9oz) shelled cooked chestnuts
75g (2¹/₂oz) unrefined sugar
25g (1oz) good-quality drinking chocolate powder
25g (1oz) dark chocolate
Pared zest of ¹/₂ orange
Pared zest of ¹/₂ tangerine
¹/₄ teaspoon mixed spice
2 cloves
1 litre (1³/₄ pints) water

Place all the ingredients in a large saucepan. Place the pan on a medium heat and bring to the boil; simmer for 30–45 minutes until the chestnuts are tender, adding more water if necessary. Serve piping hot, at any time of the day (or night).

'Duff' chestnut rum

If you've ever had the disappointment of opening chestnut husks only to find tiny or even no nuts inside the thorny shells, you might be comforted to hear that your harvest doesn't need to be wasted. The empty woody shells add a beautiful flavour so use your 'duff' harvest to turn a reasonable rum into something very special indeed.

————

MAKES 500ML (18FL OZ)
600ml (20fl oz) dark rum
150g (5oz) chestnuts
50g (2oz) butter
1 tablespoon unrefined brown sugar

Wash the chestnuts before slitting the shells and peeling as much as possible off the nuts. In a heavy pan, dissolve the butter. Place the chestnuts and their shells in the pan and, stirring continually, heat for 5 minutes until they start to release a nutty aroma. Place them in a kilner jar, pour a splash of rum into the pan to deglaze the butter, and pour into the jar, covering with the rest of the rum. Leave to infuse for at least couple of weeks before tasting, adding a spoonful of brown sugar if needed (the rum, butter and nuts will have made it sweet already).

Winter

This is the time to dig up wild roots, sweeter now than during the summer as the plants push their sugary energy stores underground to keep the roots alive during the long freeze. Grab your spade and dig up dandelions and burdock to turn into immune-boosting tonics. Should the ground be as hard as iron, there are still harvests to be had from citrus-flavoured evergreens and tender herbs like cleavers. Of course, once you come in from the cold, you should also have your wild preserved stores from the warmer months to enjoy. An autumnal fruit liqueur or a drink that tastes of the summer will remind you that warmer times are around the corner.

Rose (hip)
Rosa spp.

Rosehips vary widely, from the small oval hips of dog rose (*Rosa canina*) and the tomato-sized flattened hips of beach rose (*Rosa rugosa*) to the cultivated roses in your garden that dangle pear-shaped hips like autumnal ornaments. Just as all roses are edible, so are all rosehips; very helpful during the rationing of the Second World War in Britain, when imported fruits like oranges weren't available. British children were sent out to harvest rosehips on an industrial scale, to be turned into bottles of syrup, sipped to replace the vitamin C in their diet.

After the austerity of rationing ended and citrus fruits were imported once again, rosehips became relegated to a food for the few wild types, rather than the many. That's a shame because rosehips contain a remarkable twenty times more vitamin C than oranges. They are also crammed with vitamin E, B vitamins and a vast array of minerals, antioxidants and fatty acids. The rosehip is quite a find – used to boost immunity, soothe sore throats, reduce inflammation and treat the symptoms of conditions such as arthritis.

Edible parts: Fruits, flowers and leaves.

Harvesting: Rosehips can ripen from summer through to midwinter. Beach roses start to ripen first, while wild dog roses usually soften in early winter. Waiting for the fruit to soften will give you the best flavour, but if you want your harvest for its vitamin content, then collect them when they are red but still firm.

Pairs with: Apple, orange, vanilla, horseradish, sumac, almond, hawthorn, quince, honey, brandy and vodka.

Locations: Woodland edges and scrubland; gardens all over the world.

Caution: Rosehip seeds are covered with irritating hairs. If you eat rosehips raw, make sure to scrape away any hairs, and always pass rosehip liquid through a fine muslin to capture them and avoid them ending up in your drink. Take care when harvesting to correctly identity the hips – there are a number of toxic red berries that ripen at the same time as rosehips.

How to drink: rosehip

Each species of rose has a unique flavour – there are orange and apple flavours mixed with honey, hints of vanilla and even tomato. And in the case of burnet rose (*R. spinosissima*), chocolate. Rosehips are full of pectin and give drinks a thick quality; if you enjoy cocktails, you'll know how important mouthfeel is.

 Wine: Rosehip wine is crisp, fruity and floral, because the seeds contain tannins to help give a dry flavour. Use whole, softened hips to make your wine.

 Liqueurs: Infusing rosehips in spirits for four weeks draws out the sweetly acid flavour. Slit the skins to allow the juices to extract into the alcohol and to pull out pectin, which will add syrupy thickness. Rosehips are great with all kinds of base spirits, from neutral ones like vodka to stronger flavours such as brandy, gin and rum.

 Cordials/syrups: Rosehips make a beautiful cordial with apple juice. Use one part rosehips to three parts apple juice. Blitz the raw hips with the juice or cook until soft, then strain and dissolve in the juice the same quantity of sugar as you have liquid. Rosehip cordial is also lovely with the addition of vanilla.

 Tea: Rosehips make a delicious immune-boosting tea using fresh or dried fruit. It is best made as a decoction steeped in hot water for 20 minutes. Strain through a tea strainer lined with a square of muslin to catch the seeds.

 Fermented drinks: Rosehips love to ferment and make delicious wild sodas, often without the need for additional yeasts. Pairing rosehips with beetroot in kvass-style drinks, in kombuchas or ginger beer adds a beautiful fruit flavour.

 Vinegars: Rosehips can be used to make drinking vinegar, especially tasty when paired with sumac or rose petals.

Spiced rosehip syrup

Rosehips' orange flavour make them a perfect pair for warming spices. This syrup is a fruitier version of a classic mulling syrup – delicious stirred into hot apple juice, cider and even drizzled into glasses of sparkling wine as a very festive drink. Using whole spices in this recipe ensures a clear syrup.

_____

MAKES 300ML (¹/₂ PINT)
200g (7oz) rosehips
350ml (12fl oz) water
About 250ml (9fl oz) orange juice
Pared zest of 1 lemon
Pared zest of 1 orange
Thumb-sized piece of ginger, grated
2 cinnamon sticks
1 teaspoon allspice berries
4 cloves
2 star anise
About 250g (9oz) sugar

Thoroughly wash the rosehips, picking off any stems and discarding any that are damaged. Place them in a saucepan and add the water. Bring to the boil, then cook over a low heat until the hips have softened. Allow to cool a little, then use a stick blender to purée them. Leave to infuse for 30 minutes. Pour the purée through a sieve lined with a double layer of muslin. Measure the juice and add the same amount of orange juice.

 Pour into a saucepan and add all the remaining ingredients, with the same amount of sugar as you have total liquid – for example, 250g (9oz) of sugar to 250ml (9fl oz) of liquid. Heat gently, and as soon as the sugar has dissolved and the mixture becomes clear, turn the heat right down. Leave the spices to infuse into the liquid over the low heat for 2 hours before straining and transferring to a sterilized bottle.

Wild rosehip soda

Rosehips and apples are botanically related and taste delicious together in this probiotic-boosting drink. Fermentation also boosts the already high vitamin C levels in the hips, and a few days of bubbling creates a delicious fizzy drink to keep you well through winter (even if it's served with gin).

_____

MAKES 500ML (18FL OZ)
100g (3¹/₂oz) rosehips
500ml (18fl oz) apple juice
1 tablespoon sugar
1 teaspoon ginger bug (if needed, see page 244)

Thoroughly wash the rosehips, picking off any stems and discarding any that are damaged. Put the rosehips in a blender with 100ml (3¹/₂fl oz) of the apple juice and blend until the hips have puréed. Add the rest of the apple juice and purée again for a few seconds. Pour the liquid through a sieve lined with a double layer of muslin into a sterilized flip-top or plastic drinks bottle.

 Using a funnel, pour the sugar into the bottle, close the lid and shake the bottle to mix the sugar into the juice. Leave in a warm spot in your kitchen for a few days, turning the bottle a couple of times each day. After 3 days, the rosehip and apple juice should start to ferment, making a fizz when the lid is unscrewed. If it hasn't started to ferment, add the ginger bug and an extra teaspoon of sugar.

 Drink as soon as it becomes bubbly and fizzy. Place in the fridge to slow down fermentation.

Juniper
Juniperus spp.

Juniper is most famously known as the key flavour of gin. Its history of being infused into drinks goes back as far as the ancient Egyptian and Greek empires, when it was first added to alcohol to be drunk as a herbal treatment. Common juniper (*Juniperus communis*) likes to grow in extreme locations, especially where the soil is thin and rocky, either in the ice cold or scorching heat. If these kinds of spots aren't your idea of a fun day foraging, thankfully there's more than one edible species. Many of them grow in towns and cities, planted to provide evergreen colour. Edible species include Californian juniper (*J. californica*), creeping juniper (*J. horizontalis*), Rocky Mountain juniper (*J. scopulorum*) and east red cedar (*J. virginiana*).

If you come across one of these junipers, take a look at the round balls that may be forming on the trees – these are juniper berries, which are in fact cones (but they're so widely known as 'berries' that this is what we'll refer to them as in this book). They ripen slowly, taking up to three years to turn blue and soft, but don't despair if your juniper berries aren't ripe; you can still use the needles like other evergreens, and even the pollen in the spring.

Edible parts: Cones (berries), pollen and needles.

Harvesting: Pick juniper berries when ripe; wait until they are soft and have a powdery bloom on the outside. Lay them on trays to dry in autumn and winter. The needles can be harvested all year, the pollen in spring.

Pairs with: Thyme, lavender, mugwort, mint, rosemary, pineapple, cherry, lemon, wine, gin and beer.

Locations: Different species of juniper grow in a wide range of climates, thriving in poor, rocky soil.

Caution: Not all juniper species are edible; make sure you properly identify your tree prior to harvesting. Juniper was historically used as an abortifacient and contraceptive – avoid juniper if you are pregnant or attempting to get pregnant. Only gather sparingly from *Juniperus communis*, unless the tree is in an area with a large population of the plants, as this species is under threat due to land use change and disease.

How to drink: juniper

Juniper's distinct flavour and covering of wild yeasts make it a great ingredient for fermenting, infusing and brewing. There is so much flavour in juniper that you can often use the same berry more than once (see the recipe for Smreka, opposite).

 Wine: The tannins and yeasts in juniper make it a good berry to use in winemaking. Should you want to simply infuse a ready-made bottle of wine, take your lead from junique, a Greek drink made by soaking juniper berries in white wine; serve as an aperitif.

 Beer: Nordic and Baltic brewers make a beer called sahti, using juniper branches and berries rather than hops as the bittering agent and preservative.

 Liqueurs: While it is best known in gin, juniper is also used in a wide range of liqueurs such as jenever, a spirit from the Netherlands made with a whisky-style base. Juniper is also delicious as a supporting flavour in fruit liqueurs such as wild blueberry, pear or sloe.

 Cordials/syrups: Juniper berries and needles make a delicious non-alcoholic syrup; infuse the berries in a sugar syrup, either alone or with other botanicals. Try adding coriander, fennel, citrus peel and cardamom for a gin-influenced syrup; or cinnamon, orange peel and rosemary for a warming winter drink.

 Tea: Juniper berries and needles make delicious antioxidant-rich, anti-inflammatory teas, either as a single ingredient or with additional herbs like lemon balm, birch leaf, dandelion and nettle.

Homemade gin

Few people know that gin is simply made by flavouring a neutral grain alcohol, most often vodka. Commercial distilleries create their gins with distillation but, for those of us wanting to make a small amount, infusing botanicals (known as compound gins) is a great way to make it quickly.

What follows is less of a recipe and more of a guide. Use the juniper and some or all of the remaining flavourings, whatever takes your fancy. Start by making smaller bottles of your infusion, and remember to write down your exact quantities and timings so that you can make it again.

————

MAKES 500ML (18FL OZ)
550ml (19fl oz) vodka
2 tablespoons juniper berries, crushed
4 cardamom pods, crushed
1/4 teaspoon coriander seeds
1/2 teaspoon Sichuan peppercorns
1/2 teaspoon black peppercorns
1 teaspoon dried rose petals
1/2 teaspoon dried lavender flowers
1 edible evergreen sprig (juniper, spruce, fir or pine)
Dried peel of 1/4 orange, lemon or grapefruit

Place the vodka in a wide-necked jar and add the juniper and cardamom, if using. Seal the jar and leave to steep overnight.

The next day, taste the vodka. If the juniper flavour is strong enough, remove the berries; if not, leave them in. Add any other flavouring ingredients you are using, seal and leave to infuse for another 10 hours.

Check the flavour again and leave to infuse for another 10 hours if the flavour is not strong enough.

Strain out the flavourings and bottle – this gin will keep for up to a year, but it is best drunk young.

Smreka (fermented juniper drink)

Smreka is a fermented juniper drink that originates in the Balkans. At its simplest, it's a non-carbonated drink made from juniper, lemons and water. You can add other ingredients to the drink – sloes, rosehips or slices of apple give a more fruity flavour. Once you have strained the drink, you can reuse the berries up to two more times to make more batches, making maximum use of the berries, their flavour and natural yeasts.

————

MAKES 1 LITRE (1³/₄ PINTS)
25g (1oz) juniper berries
1/2 unwaxed lemon, sliced
1 litre (1³/₄ pints) unchlorinated water
Sugar (optional)
Honey, to serve

Place the berries, lemon and water in a wide-necked jar, seal and leave in a warm room to ferment for 7–14 days. Taste after 7 days – it should be tangy and refreshing. Once it's to your liking, strain the liquid into a sterilized bottle and store in the fridge for up to 2 weeks.

If you want to make the drink fizzy, add a dessertspoon of sugar to the bottle and leave at room temperature for a few days until sparkling, then store in the fridge.

You can drink this neat with honey to sweeten, or dilute it with sparkling water or fruit juice (pineapple and apple are both delicious).

Burdock
Arctium spp.

First fermented hundreds of years ago as a herbal medicinal drink, dandelion and burdock has (rather sadly) evolved over time into the fizzy drink full of sugars or sweeteners found in soft drinks aisles today. Burdock and dandelions were first made into drinks because of a special ingredient they share called inulin. Inulin is a prebiotic fibre that supports gut health, controls blood sugar, and is even used to control diabetes. Burdock is also rich in antioxidants; it is used as a blood purifier, supports the liver to rid the blood of toxins, and aids the kidneys by acting as a diuretic.

Burdock is a biennial plant that forms a rosette of downy leaves with a large, long tap root in the first year. In its second year, it produces tall flowering stems with sticky seedheads or burrs. The leaves have an aromatic covering which smells sweet, but is actually extremely bitter to eat (making it perfect for bitters). Dig up young clumps with their thick roots in the winter after their first year of growth to brew into delicious dandelion and burdock, and you'll never have to visit that fizzy drinks aisle again.

Edible parts: Roots, leaves, young flower stems, flowers and seeds (making sure to rub away any irritating hairs from around the seeds).

Harvesting: Dig up roots from winter until early spring after the plant's first year of growth, before the tall flowering stems appear. Burdock roots snap easily; using a long spade helps to dig up more roots. The leaves can be harvested all year, the flowering stems in spring and the flowers and seeds in summer.

Pairs with: Dandelion, juniper, star anise, carrot, ginger, dark brown sugar, liquorice, gin and rum.

Locations: Footpaths, roadways and areas with disturbed soil.

Caution: Take care using burdock if you are allergic to the daisy (Asteraceae) family. In the first year, burdock looks similar to butterbur (*Petasites*) and foxglove (*Digitalis*); learn the difference between the three plants before harvesting.

How to drink: burdock

The leaves and stems of burdock are covered in an aromatic bitter substance, making them an ideal bittering flavouring for cocktails. The roots have a bitter skin, but once it's peeled back, it reveals a sweet earthy flavour, which is intensified when roasted.

 Beer: Dandelion and burdock beer is a lightly fermented beer with an earthy, warming flavour.

 Liqueurs: Craft distillers blend dandelion and burdock syrup with gin to make a delicious sweet liqueur. Burdock roots are also lovely infused into spiced rum.

 Spirits: Pocketful of Stones distillery in Cornwall, England, adds burdock roots to their gin, giving the drink an earthy, bitter flavour.

 Coffee: Burdock roots are beneficial and delicious ingredients in root coffees – try them blended with chicory and dandelion roots.

 Warming/milky drinks: Burdock roots are also delicious in chais with chicory and dandelion roots and warming spices.

 Bitters/tinctures: Burdock bitters can be made in combination with other herbs and spices or as a single-ingredient bitter – especially the aromatic leaves. You can also serve pieces of leaf with cocktails for your guests to infuse in their own drinks, removing when the drink is bitter enough for their taste buds.

Dandelion & burdock beer

Unlike the bottles in the soft drinks aisles, homemade dandelion and burdock beer is slightly alcoholic and very easy to drink.

_____

MAKES 2 LITRES (3½ PINTS)
150g (5oz) burdock roots
50g (2oz) dandelion roots
2 litres (3½ pints) water
500g (1lb 2oz) soft brown sugar
1 star anise
2 tablespoons treacle
Juice of 1 lemon
1 sachet of brewer's yeast, about 5g (⅛oz)

Thoroughly scrub the roots before slicing finely and placing them both in a saucepan. Add the water and boil for 30 minutes.

Stir in the sugar, star anise, treacle and lemon juice, simmer for a further 5 minutes, then leave to cool down to room temperature.

Strain the liquid into a sterilized fermenting container and stir in the yeast. Cover and leave at room temperature for up to a week, or until the drink starts bubbling. Transfer to sterilized bottles and release the pressure on the bottles every day if it is very bubbly. The drink will change flavour over the next few days; taste it every couple of days and when you have a pleasant balance of sweet, sour and earthy, put the bottles in the fridge and drink within a few days.

Burdock & pomegranate amaro

Burdock roots provide the perfect warming backbone for bittersweet liqueurs. The edible peel of pomegranates is astringent and tart. Both plants are in season through the winter and pair to make a perfect digestif for after a meal. Use as high grade a base spirit as you can find to help draw out the flavours in the botanicals.

_____

MAKES 500ML (18FL OZ)
400ml (14fl oz) vodka
2 tablespoons fresh burdock root, finely chopped
Peel and pith from ½ pomegranate
1 burdock leaf
10 rosemary leaves
5 sage leaves
5 mint leaves
Peel of 1 organic orange
10 fennel seeds
Seeds from 1 pomegranate
150g (5oz) sugar
500ml (18fl oz) water

Place all the ingredients, apart from the pomegranate seeds, sugar and water in a jar. Press the ingredients under the spirit, cover and leave to macerate for 24 hours before straining.

Place the pomegranate seeds, sugar and water in a saucepan, bring to the boil, then simmer for 20 minutes. Steep for 1 hour before straining the syrup through a sieve lined with muslin. Blend the spirit with equal amounts of the syrup, adding more if you would like a sweeter drink. Pour into a sterilized bottle and drink within 2 months. Serve neat over ice, or in a cocktail.

Dandelion
Taraxacum spp.

In the spring, dandelion flowers open in succession, turning fields and verges yellow before they turn into moon-like seedheads, filling the air with tiny parachutes of seeds, blown away to put down roots elsewhere. Through the rest of the year, the bitter nutritious leaves and thick tap roots are important ingredients in any wild drinks larder. Get to know dandelions in spring when in their blaze of golden glory and you'll be equipped to return later in the year to harvest the leaves and dig up their roots.

Dandelion leaves can vary; some are toothed like lions' teeth (hence the French name *dent-de-lion*, meaning tooth of the lion), while others are less obviously so. The roots are full of gut-supporting inulin and are used medicinally to support and detoxify the liver. The flowers aren't only good for identification purposes; they too are edible – deliciously honeyed with high levels of immune-supporting polyphenols. They make rather ambrosial wines and syrups.

Edible parts: Roots, leaves, flowers and flower stems. The seeds can be sprouted.

Harvesting: Harvest dandelion roots from late autumn through to spring. The majority of the flowers appear during a short season in spring, but there will still be a few opening through the summer. The leaves can be harvested all year, but look for tender, fresh growth.

Pairs with: Roots: with burdock root, barley, rye, chicory, star anise, cinnamon, chocolate, coffee, cream, rum, whisky and brandy. Leaves: with nettle, orange, rosemary, pine needles, lemon and cleavers. Flowers: with citrus, cream and chocolate.

Locations: Almost all unploughed grasslands; dandelions prefer open sunny sites.

How to drink: dandelion

Different parts of dandelion have their own distinct flavours – honeyed flowers; bitter, fresh and minerally leaves; and warming, chocolatey roots. Pairing different parts of the plant blends together their flavours, for example, sweetening dandelion root coffee with a syrup made from the flowers.

 Wine: Dandelion flower wine is honeyed, citrusy and floral – for the best results, collect your petals on the morning that you make your wine.

 Liqueurs: The flowers and roots both make good liqueurs. Infuse the flowers for a couple of hours in a neutral spirit to extract the honeyed flavour and create a drink that you can sweeten with a small amount of sugar and vanilla. The roots can be used raw or roasted for a deeper flavour and the resulting liqueur sweetened with dandelion flower syrup or a light honey.

 Cordials/syrups: Harvest freshly opened flowers to infuse into syrups and cordials. Snip the petals from the green centre to remove bitter flavours. Dandelion flower cordial is especially lovely made with oranges.

 Tea: The leaves, flowers and roots can all be used as tea. The leaves and flowers are best used as cold infusions, the roots made as a hot infusion or decoction.

 Coffee: Roasted roots ground into a powder can be made into what is known as dandelion coffee. It's also delicious as an ingredient in chai drinks, especially with spices like cinnamon and clove.

 Fermented drinks: The flowers make a light wild soda. Fill a wide-necked 1 litre (1¾ pint) jar with petals, add 200g (7oz) of sugar and cover with cooled boiled water. Leave for a few days, stirring each day. If you don't have any bubbles by then, add a pinch of wine yeast. Sieve the liquid from the petals and pour into a plastic bottle. After two days, the bottle should become tight and the drink will be fizzy. It can be drunk immediately or left to ferment further, becoming slightly sour.

 Bitters/tinctures: Both the leaves and roots can be used in bitters. The leaves add an astringent green bitterness, the roots a woody warming flavour.

Dandelion root coffee

Dandelion coffee is dark and mellow in flavour. It doesn't contain caffeine, but instead is packed full of gut- and liver-supporting inulin, well worth the lack of the stimulant. Harvest the roots during winter or early spring. Although they will shrink during cooking, you'll have an additional bonus harvest of leaves. These can be dried into teas, making the digging even more worthwhile.

————————
MAKES 150G (5OZ)
1kg (2lb 4oz) dandelion roots

Wash, then cut the dandelion roots into pea-sized pieces, spread out in a single layer on a baking tray lined with baking paper and place in an oven at 50°C (122°F), leaving the door slightly ajar. If your oven doesn't go this low, place them on a radiator or in a dehydrator. Leave the roots in the oven for 2 hours to dry.

Once the roots feel dry, turn the oven up to 180°C (350°F), Gas Mark 4, and toast the roots until they turn dark brown and are completely dry. Depending on your oven and the size of the pieces of root, this could take 20–40 minutes, so keep checking them.

When the roots are roasted, remove them from the oven and grind into a fine powder with a coffee grinder. Store in a jar until needed.

To make a cup of coffee, place 1 heaped tablespoon per person in a cafetière, pour over boiling water and brew for 10 minutes. Serve black or with milk and sweeten as desired.

Dandelion flower wine

Dandelion flower wine is light and honeyed, with a very subtle bitter flavour. Make sure only to use the petals, snipping them away from the base of the flower.

————————
MAKES 5 LITRES (8³/₄ PINTS)
4.5 litres (8 pints) water
1kg (2lb 4oz) white sugar
120g (4oz) dandelion petals (snipped from the flowerheads)
Pared zest and juice of 2 unwaxed lemons
1 Campden tablet, crumbled
1 sachet of Champagne yeast, about 5g (¹/₈oz)

Sterilize all your equipment just before you use it (see page 233). Place the water in a large saucepan and bring to the boil. Add the sugar and stir until it has dissolved. Let the sugar water cool until just warm.

Meanwhile, place the petals, lemon juice and zest in a sterilized bucket. Pour the sweetened water over the flowers and add the crumbled Campden tablet. Cover the floral mixture and leave for 24 hours.

Stir in the Champagne yeast, cover the bucket again and leave until bubbles start appearing, stirring a couple of times a day to press the flowers under the liquid.

Once the mixture is bubbling, strain the liquid into a sterilized demijohn (or other container on which you can fit an airlock). When the bubbling has stopped (after about 3 weeks), siphon the wine into a second demijohn and leave for 6 months to mature. Transfer to sterilized bottles and drink young (it's not a wine that improves with age).

Douglas fir
Pseudotsuga menziesii

Douglas firs are evergreen conifers and, like the other conifer trees featured in this book, have citrus-flavoured needles. If you rub them, you'll release a potent grapefruit perfume – even in the middle of winter, the soft needles have this fresh, vibrant scent and taste. A mature tree can often grow over 50m (165ft) tall but, fortunately, around the base, you'll often find small saplings to harvest from. If you are harvesting from unlabelled trees, look for key features to identify the correct species.

The trunks of mature trees are deeply cracked and often have blisters full of sticky resin. The pine cones are distinctive, made up of scales with three pointed bracts hanging from their bases. The needles are flat, green on top and silvery on the underside with two pale green, almost white, lines running along their lengths. You might also see buds at the ends of the branches; these are pointy and wrapped in a brown papery sticky coating. Lastly, rub the needles to make sure they smell like grapefruit and Christmas all in one.

Edible parts: Shoots, needles, cones, seeds and resin (as an extract in small amounts).

Harvesting: You can harvest Douglas fir all year, from the tender shoots in spring to older needles throughout winter. When you pick the needles, cut away any brown parts that join the twigs; these are bitter and resinous. The resin from a blister can be collected into little pots.

Pairs with: Lemon, grapefruit, rosemary, sage, yuzu, lemongrass, tangerine, smoke, gin, vodka, maple syrup and molasses.

Locations: Douglas fir grows in parks, large gardens and woodlands, often in commercial forests growing as a timber crop.

Caution: Deadly poisonous yew is a member of the conifer family and has flat needles like Douglas fir. Fortunately, yew doesn't have the two pale lines on the undersides of the needles; the needles don't grow around the twigs (like Douglas fir does) or smell of grapefruit. Check these things as a guide for identification.

How to drink: Douglas fir

Douglas fir's grapefruit flavour is intense but the older winter needles need some effort to give it up: pounding, blitzing or heating the needles helps to break open their beautiful flavour. In the spring, revisit your tree to harvest the soft, tender new needles that need far less work. You can simply scatter them into drinks (or food).

Beer: Brewed like Spruce tip beer (see page 217), Douglas fir beer has flavours that are similar to citral beers.

Liqueurs: Soaked in spirits and sweetened with sugar or honey, Douglas fir liqueurs are beautiful to drink by themselves or can be used in cocktails.

Cordials/syrups: Make cordial by infusing young shoots or older needles in syrup (older needles have an additional vanilla flavour). Green cones can be used like Scots pine cones to make a version of mugolio (see page 43).

Tea: Rich in vitamin C, Douglas fir not only tastes good but is good for you. Use the young needles and shoots in cold water or hot water infusions, the older needles in decoction teas.

Fermented drinks: Like its edible evergreen counterparts, douglas fir needles and cones are great added to fermented drinks like wild soda (see Pine needle soda on page 43) kombucha and tepache drinks.

Salts/sugars: Blend the needles with salt or sugar to make grapefruit-flavoured finishing salt and sugar.

Bitters/tinctures: The sticky resin is incredibly potent and usually used for its antiseptic properties. Slowly macerated into alcohol, it will create a very strong flavouring but use it sparingly – a single drop will be enough to add an evergreen taste to drinks.

Douglas fir, orange peel & rosemary decoction tea

By midwinter, our immune systems are waning and circulation is sluggish. This warming, simmered tea is full of anti-inflammatory, circulation-boosting and soothing properties and a good dose of immune-boosting vitamin C. As if it wasn't good enough already, Douglas fir needles are traditionally used to treat colds and respiratory infections and, as you heat your tea, your house will be filled with the wonderful scents.

————

MAKES 50G (2OZ)
30g (1oz) Douglas fir needles, brown ends removed
10g (¹/₄oz) rosemary leaves
Peel of 2 organic oranges, chopped
1 teaspoon ground star anise

Place the fir needles, rosemary leaves and orange peel in a dehydrator and dry until the orange is brittle. Place the mixture in a jar, add the star anise, seal and shake to distribute a dusting of the spice through the other ingredients.

    To make the decoction, place a good pinch of tea per person in a small saucepan and cover with 350ml (12fl oz) of water per person. Place the pan on a low heat and simmer for 20 minutes before straining and serving. Sweeten with maple syrup or honey if desired.

Douglas fir & grapefruit negroni bianco

It's not just children who can have fun at Christmas – choose a Douglas fir for your festive tree and (if you know it hasn't been sprayed with any toxic chemicals) you can snip off a bit for yourself to make a cocktail. You really ought to share this with Santa, but probably won't.

————

SERVES 4
20g (³/₄oz) Douglas fir needles, brown ends removed
1 teaspoon sugar
150ml (5fl oz) gin
2 large ice cubes
120ml (4fl oz) dry vermouth
120ml (4fl oz) bitter bianco
4 strips of fresh grapefruit peel, each about 5cm (2in) long
2 sprigs of Douglas fir, to decorate

Place the needles in a non-porous mortar, add the sugar with a splash of the gin and grind with the pestle until they start to break down. Pour over the rest of the gin and let the needles infuse for 1 hour.

    Strain the gin into two cocktail glasses, each containing a large piece of ice. Add the vermouth and bitter bianco, slip a stirrer between the ice and glass and stir the ingredients for 20 seconds until they are fully mixed. Take the grapefruit peel and twist it above the glasses to release its (Douglas fir-like) oils. Push the peel into the glasses and decorate each with a sprig of Douglas fir.

Spruce
Picea spp.

When most other trees have lost their leaves in the winter, the evergreens hold onto their vitamin C-rich needles, giving access to nutrients and a delicious citrus flavour at a time when locally fresh food is less than easy to come by in cooler climates. Just as edible Douglas firs are cut down as Christmas trees each year, so millions of spruces are chopped to decorate homes with their far sharper needles. As the needles inevitably start dropping all over your floor, shake a few into a jar – you have ready-made spruce tip tea, full of vitamins and a mellow pine, vanilla, woody flavour.

Should your tree have its roots still, plant it outside once it's been stripped of its decor and you'll find in spring that it is decorated once again, this time with a brown papery bauble perched on the tip of each branch. As the rounded balls swell, the paper falls away, uncovering vibrant green new shoots – spruce tips. For a fleeting moment these tender tips are soft enough to eat – astringent, lemony with a hint of peel – and perfect for making beers and sodas so delicious that you'll never want to chop a spruce down again.

Edible parts: Needles, bark and cones.

Harvesting: Spruce can be harvested all year; the soft tips emerge in mid spring. Snipping off the ends of twigs makes it easier to carry the needles into the kitchen – young shoots fall apart easily, so put them straight into a tub or bag without holes when you harvest them.

Pairs with: Lemon, orange, quince, apple, pear, plum, blackberry, sloe, walnut, vanilla, nettle, fennel, rosemary, blackcurrant (fruit and leaf), wine, gin, brandy and rum.

Locations: Coniferous woodland, gardens and parkland.

How to drink: spruce

As spruce needles harden, their flavour takes longer to extract into a liquid – treat young tips as a tender herb, but the older, woodier needles like a dry ingredient or woody spice, leaving them longer in water or alcohol to infuse.

Wine: Country winemakers use the new tips to make a unique fresh wine which is dry and astringent with a citrus flavour.

Tea: Pair with rosehips and hawthorn for a fruity, warming winter tea. In spring, the tips are delicious with flowering currant and nettles.

Beer: Spruce beer can be made with the young tips or older needles. Either ferment lightly as a soda or use as citrus flavouring in grain-based beers and ales.

Fermented drinks: Young spruce tips make delicious wild sodas, especially when you add a yeast-rich green spruce cone into your mixture. The older needles are lovely added to kombuchas or ginger beers, and South American tepache drinks.

Liqueurs: Spruce needles are lovely turned into liqueurs all alone, but are also very good pushed into bottles of sloe gin or damson vodka.

Salts/sugars: Grind spruce needles with salt into a powder for a wonderful finisher for a Martini glass.

Cordials/syrups: Try infusing the needles in sugar syrup with clementine zest for a tasty winter cordial.

Spruce tip beer

Once spruce beer was widely consumed. Brewed for its health benefits, spruce was often part of a ship's food cargo, providing vitamin C while at sea. Spruce tip beer is usually made with young shoots in the spring, but also works with older needles – just make sure they are fresh rather than dried.

_____

MAKES 10 X 330ML (11FL OZ) BOTTLES
3 litres (5¼ pints) water
Thumb-sized piece of root ginger, finely chopped
10g (¼oz) dried hops
40g (1¼oz) spruce needles
360g (12½oz) malt extract
1 sachet of brewer's yeast, about 5g (⅛oz)

Place the water in a large saucepan and bring to the boil. Add the ginger, hops and spruce and boil for 30 minutes, then add the malt extract and boil for a further 10 minutes.

Strain the liquid and allow it to cool to room temperature – about 21°C (70°F) – before stirring in the yeast. Pour into a sterilized fermenting vessel, cover and leave for 1 week before transferring to sterilized bottles. This beer can be drunk straight away (which is lucky if you're on a long voyage on a tall ship that has run out of fruit and veg).

Spruce, quince & rose sour

Perfumed quinces are a real winter treat and beautiful paired with edible evergreens. If you don't have access to a crop of quinces, swap them for the sourest apples you can find (crab apples are perfect). This is one of the best non-alcoholic cocktails you can hand your friends, but should you wish to make the drink more fortifying, you could always add a measure or two of gin.

_____

SERVES 2
2 quinces (or 4 very sour apples)
500ml (18fl oz) water
Juice of ½ lemon
20g (¾oz) spruce needles
1 tablespoon simple sugar syrup
½ teaspoon rose water or the petals from
   a frozen fragrant rose
2 spruce twigs, to decorate

Wash the quinces to remove any fluff on the skin. Roughly chop the fruit and place into a saucepan or slow cooker (skin and seeds included) with the water and lemon juice. Cover and cook on a low heat (or high setting on the slow cooker) until the fruit turns amber and collapses.

Use a potato masher to pulp the fruit, then add the spruce needles and leave to infuse for a few hours. Strain the pulpy liquid through a jelly bag or a large sieve lined with muslin, letting the liquid drip out. Don't be tempted to squeeze out the liquid or it will be cloudy. The pulp can be discarded or used to make membrillo.

Fill a cocktail shaker with ice, pour in the quince and spruce mixture and add the syrup and rose water. Shake and strain into cocktail glasses, distributing any foam between the drinks, then decorate with spruce twigs.

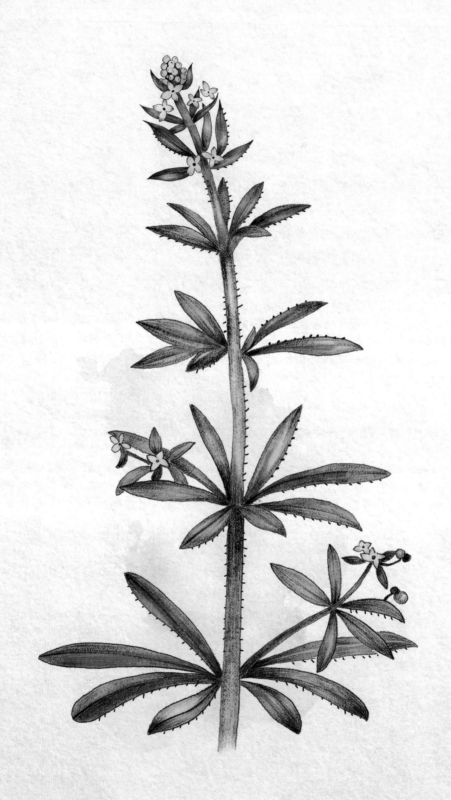

Cleavers or catchweed
Galium aparine

Young cleavers climb up through hedges, their lance-shaped leaves growing in whorls like spokes of a wheel along the plant's square stems. They are prolific annual plants that you're most likely to notice in the summer, when they smother hedges and shrubs with long, rope-like, bristled stems that stick to everything like fuzzy felt. If you see a hedge covered in cleavers, head back in the winter and you'll find its offspring starting to grow. By early summer they'll be sporting tiny white flowers that, when pollinated, produce seed that can be gathered and roasted.

It's not just the seeds of cleavers that are edible – return to that hedgerow throughout the winter and spring to harvest the new year's green tender growth. Cleavers stems and leaves are a herbal superhero, used as a tonic to cleanse lymphatic systems, which, during the hibernation of winter, can get sluggish. Infusing them in water overnight will provide you with a hydrating tonic drink that tastes of fresh cucumber – just the drink to have after your (cleavers) coffee.

Edible parts: Leaves, stems and seeds.

Harvesting: Pick the stems from autumn to late spring. Use scissors to harvest the shoots to avoid pulling up the muddy roots. Once the plant forms flowers in the summer, stop harvesting and allow the seeds to form. Collect the seeds once they are ripe and turning brown by placing the long stems into bags (paper or plastic) and shaking so that they drop into the bag.

Pairs with: Cucumber, pea, celery, rhubarb, juniper, ginger, melon, apple, nettle, lemon and gin.

Locations: Hedgerows, fences, garden vegetable and flower beds.

Caution: Cleavers are best taken in moderation and avoided by pregnant women. Some people can have a dermatitis reaction when handling cleavers – if you have one, it is advised not to consume them. If drying cleavers, ensure they are dried quickly and thoroughly to prevent dangerous moulds that can affect the blood.

How to drink: cleavers

The fresh flavour and health-boosting benefits of cleavers turn it from a nuisance weed to a longed-for friend. It has cooling properties, so if you have a cold constitution then pair the herb with warming spices like ginger or horseradish.

Liqueurs: Cleavers' herbal tones make it a natural ally in herbal liqueurs. Cleavers are now found in artisan gins, lending a much-desired grassy sweetness.

Tea: Cleavers are traditionally made into tea, using either hot or cold water. Steeping in cold water overnight draws out the fresh cucumber overtones, creating a thirst-quenching drink.

Coffee: Harvest the brown seeds to toast and make a lightly caffeinated coffee substitute. Use a good-quality grinder that can deal with these incredibly hard seeds.

Fermented drinks: Combine cleavers with herb-like nettles to make delicious beers.

Salts/sugars: Soak handfuls of cleavers overnight in a salt solution made from 1 teaspoon of salt to 100ml (3½fl oz) of water. Dry the salt-soaked cleavers and grind with a teaspoon of salt to make a gently herbal finishing salt for cocktails. The leftover brine can be used in Dirty Martinis.

Juice: Cleavers juice can be used as a tonic shot, much like wheatgrass, using a splash of water to help extract the juice from the plant (herbalists recommend taking no more than 2 tablespoons per day). Blending with celery, ginger and apple juice makes a vibrant, fresh, cucumber-flavoured juice drink.

Cleavers & celery tonic juice

Cleavers complement celery and share its nourishing, cleansing properties, making them an ideal pairing in a detoxifying juice drink.

―――――――

SERVES 1
20g (³/₄oz) young cleavers (leaves and stems)
Thumb-sized piece of fresh root ginger,
  finely chopped
2 celery sticks
250ml (9fl oz) apple juice

Wash and roughly chop the cleavers, then juice them in a juicer along with the ginger and celery. Add the apple juice and enjoy. The leftover pulp can then be added to soups such as watercress or nettle.

Cleavers coffee

Cleaver seeds can be roasted and turned into the closest substitute for coffee you'll find because they are in the same botanical family as coffee, even containing a small amount of caffeine.

―――――――

MAKES A 200ML (7FL OZ) JAR
100g (3¹/₂oz) cleaver seeds

First, rub the seeds in a sieve to break away any debris. Spread out the cleaned seeds on a baking tray and place in a preheated oven at 160°C (325°F), Gas Mark 3. Roast the seeds for 30 minutes, give the seeds a shake and roast for another 15–30 minutes until grey-brown and sweet smelling, checking to make sure they don't burn.

Place the seeds in a coffee or spice grinder and grind into a powder. Use 1 heaped teaspoon per person, brewing the coffee for 10 minutes before straining through a coffee filter. You can drink the coffee by itself or with chai-inspired spices.

Maple

Acer spp.

Maple trees range from the sugar maples of North America to sycamores and slender acers. While the sugar maple is the best known for providing sap to be turned into syrup, many of the other maples offer us sap too, as well as other ingredients to eat and drink. The leaves, blossoms, seeds and even inner bark are all edible offerings from maple trees, and many of these are just as moreish as the syrup.

You probably have a bottle of maple syrup in your kitchen, or perhaps in your drinks cabinet, as it makes a sweet partner for cocktails, especially those with a rich flavour and bases of whisky, brandy or rum. It is made by reducing the watery, barely sweet sap that flows around trees as the weather starts to warm – it takes 30 litres of sap to make 1 litre of syrup. The sap is actually a drink in itself, either consumed like water or brewed into beer, wine or mead. Maple sap is harvested with metal taps or spiles, which drip the liquid into buckets for a few weeks each year. Commercial maple groves look far from romantic, with miles of plastic lines drawing the sap from hundreds of trees into huge evaporation tanks.

Edible parts: Sap, leaves, flowers, seeds and inner bark.

Harvesting: Sap is usually harvested by tapping into the trunk of the tree at the end of winter. A less intrusive way is to break the end of a branch and push a bottle onto it; you'll get less sap, but there's less risk of damaging the tree. Collect blossoms in the late spring when just opened and dripping in sticky sap. Maple leaves are usually gathered early in the spring or in the autumn when they have turned red and are full of beneficial compounds.

Pairs with: Apple, cinnamon, vanilla, milk, butter, nut liqueurs, peach, nutmeg, cider, whisky, bourbon, rum, spruce and beech leaves.

Locations: Depending on the species, maples can be found in woodlands (including sugar maple and sycamore) or gardens (including Japanese maple).

Caution: American *Acer negundo* or box elder has a long history of being tapped for its sap, but unlike other maples, its seeds are toxic.

How to drink: maple

Different species of maple have slightly different flavours and beneficial properties (sycamore syrup, for example, tastes like macadamia nuts). Experiment with the different species growing locally to you.

The sap, known as maple water, contains phytonutrients, vitamins, minerals and antioxidants. It is faintly sweet but incredibly refreshing, making it a perfect sports drink. Sap ferments quickly and turns sour so to preserve your sap at peak flavour, store it in the freezer until needed (leaving space in the container for expansion as the liquid freezes).

 Wine: Maple wine is often made with the final sap of the season, which tends to be bitter and sour. It makes a dry, crisp wine that needs the addition of extra syrup or other sugar, tannins and acidity; the sap is often added to a grape concentrate to make a fruity wine. You can also use maple blossoms to make a floral wine.

 Beer: Like wine, the last harvest of maple sap from a season is often turned into beer as it is better suited to brewing rather than turning into sweet sugar syrup.

 Cordials/syrups: Syrup made from the start and middle of the maple-tapping season is often amber, sweet and light. The later-collected sap makes dark maple syrup, which is more like molasses in flavour. Rich in minerals and vitamins, maple syrup is the perfect sweetener for hot toddies.

 Tea: Maple syrup or sugar is often added to black tea leaves in Canada to make a sweet black tea. In Japan, the leaves of the nikko maple have a long history of being used as a herbal tea; more recently the amber leaves of Japanese maple have been used by pioneering company Maple Laboratory. Maple blossoms can also be used in herbal teas to provide sweetness, wonderful blended with mint and lemon balm.

 Fermented drinks: Saps ferment very quickly, usually without any additional yeast, and will create a fizzy drink in a few days. Add additional sugars – honey, light brown sugar or, of course, maple syrup work well. The blossoms of maple also make wild sodas. Maple syrup added to honey in mead-making creates an amber mead known as acerglyn (see opposite).

Maple mead (acerglyn)

Acerglyn is a mead made with a combination of maple syrup and honey, with the addition of spices and oranges; it is a perfect warming drink for after a cold day harvesting maple sap at the end of winter.

MAKES 5 LITRES (8³/₄ PINTS)
1 cinnamon stick
375ml (13fl oz) maple syrup
375ml (13fl oz) honey
4.5 litres (8 pints) water
1 unwaxed orange, cut into wedges (with peel)
1 sachet of Champagne yeast, about 5g (¹/₈oz)

Place the cinnamon, syrup and honey in a heavy-based saucepan and heat until the honey and syrup melt. Add 1 litre (1³/₄ pints) of the water and simmer for 15 minutes before removing from the heat and allowing to cool.

Pour the cooled liquid into a sterilized demijohn and add the orange wedges. Pour over the rest of the water, stir with the end of a sterilized spoon, then use a funnel to add the Champagne yeast and stir again. Place on the airlock and leave in a warm room at about 23°C (73.5°F) to ferment for 2–4 weeks, until it stops bubbling.

Transfer the mead to sterilized bottles. You can drink it straight away but maple mead is best after a few months of maturing. Store for up to 6 months.

Maple blossom, cucumber & mint cooler

Maple blossoms change in flavour from vegetal when in bud to honeyed and sweet as the flowers open. You can make this cocktail with unopened or opened flowers, just adjust the sweetener according to how much sweetness is already on the blossoms. Leaving out the gin will create an equally beautiful non-alcoholic drink.

SERVES 2
8 maple or 4 sycamore blossoms
90ml (3fl oz) gin
10 mint leaves
10cm (4in) piece of peeled cucumber, grated
Juice of ¹/₂ lime
2 teaspoons light maple syrup or simple sugar syrup
Ice cubes
225ml (8fl oz) tonic water or seltzer

Place half the maple blossoms in a cocktail shaker, add the gin and leave to soak for 30 minutes.

Add the mint leaves, grated cucumber, lime and syrup. Muddle (smash) the ingredients together before filling the shaker with ice. Shake vigorously. Curl the remaining maple blossoms in the bottoms of two glasses, add ice and strain over the drink. Top up with tonic or seltzer.

Camellia
Camellia spp.

The one plant in this book you probably drink on a regular basis is camellia – or more specifically *Camellia sinensis*, the tea plant. Tea was originally drunk, so they say, thousands of years ago by the father of Chinese herbal medicine, emperor Shennong. Over the millennia, *Camellia sinensis* has become so associated with tea that tea aficionados can get rather irate if you call another plant tea, even if it's another camellia. Which is a shame because *C. sinensis* isn't the only member of its family to make a good brew.

Unlike the tender *C. sinensis*, which likes to be mollycoddled on warm slopes, other types of camellia, including *C. japonica*, are hardier things and more likely to be growing near you if you live in cooler climates. Whether you have a tender sinensis plant with its papery white flowers, or a shiny thick-leaved japonica with bright winter blooms, you can make your own tea using the unfurling buds and young or even older tougher leaves. And you can even brew tea using your camellia's abundance of flowers, making a winter floral tea (or tisane if you're a tea pedant).

Edible parts: Leaves, flowers and seeds (used to make an edible oil).

Harvesting: Pick the flowers on a dry day. They bruise easily, so put them into a tub to avoid getting bashed. The leaves can be collected when in bud to make a white tea, the young leaves are used to make a green-style tea and the older leaves to make a black tea. Camellia leaves can become dusty, so wash them after picking.

Pairs with: Nettle, magnolia, honeysuckle, osmanthus flower, jasmine, mint, lemon, cardamom, clove, cinnamon, rum, brandy, whisky and gin.

Locations: Gardens and parks in dappled shade.

How to drink: camellia

Just as tea doesn't have to be made from *Camellia sinensis*, so camellias don't have to just be teas – the subtly astringent and bitter, floral and fresh flavours of the leaves and flowers are beautiful in a wide range of drinks, hot and cold.

Wine: Both the flowers and leaves can be brewed into wines. Winemaker Copenhagen Organic make a range of low-alcohol sparkling green tea wine. Experiment with your leaves by using them fresh or fermented for different flavours.

Liqueurs: Both the leaves and flowers of camellia can be infused into spirits to make liqueurs. Portugal has a long association with camellias and a number of distilleries today make a sweet liqueur using camellia flowers grown locally. Tea leaf liqueurs can be made by brewing tea (homemade or otherwise) in cold water overnight, before straining and adding to a neutral spirit. Leave to infuse for a couple of days before sweetening.

Cordials/syrups: Make camellia flower or leaf syrups to add to cocktails and iced teas by making a strong tea before adding the same quantity of sugar as liquid. Leaves are lovely paired with lemon zest, the flowers with jasmine, magnolia or osmanthus flowers.

Tea: Tannin and caffeine content varies – some species will give you a light floral brew, others like *Camellia sinensis* a more tannic, astringent drink. More delicate teas are best drunk black. The flowers are also used in teas – golden camellia flower tea is a revered floral tea from the *Camellia chrysantha* shrub, but any camellia flower can be used in teas with other botanicals or alone.

Fermented drinks: Tea is linked to fermented probiotic drinks such as kombucha and jun. Try using black tea (homemade or bought) in the first fermentation, followed by handfuls of camellia flowers in the second to add a floral, lightly spiced flavour.

Bitters: Make bitters to go with dark spirits by infusing black tea leaves with birch or oak twigs, or with earthy flavours like burdock (very good in Old Fashioned cocktails). Green leaves make bitters that elevate gin – try making them with fresh camellia leaves paired with cardamom, mahonia bark and lemon or yuzu zest.

Camellia leaf tea

All camellias can be used to make tea with their leaves – *C. japonica*, for example, makes a mild, almost floral tea. Harvesting at different stages of growth, and processing in various ways, will give you a selection of different types of tea from one plant.

White tea
To make an equivalent to white tea, harvest the young leaf buds as they start to unfurl in the spring. Break them open and dry them as they are for a delicate grassy flavour.

Green tea
Make a green tea by harvesting the young, fully opened leaves at the ends of the leaf stems. Gather in the morning when their flavour is at its height and lay on a tea towel somewhere warm to wither for a few hours. Place the withered leaves in a warm wok, making sure to keep agitating the leaves so they don't burn. Once they are hot, remove them from the pan and roll into tight cigars before placing in a low oven or dehydrator to dry out completely.

Black tea
For black tea, allow the leaves to wither overnight then break open the cell walls with a rolling pin, or by rolling back and forth in tight cigars. Lay the leaves out in a warm room (an airing cupboard is ideal) – the leaves will oxidize and slowly turn brown. Once totally brown, dry the leaves in a dehydrator or low oven.

Camellia flower tea

Camellia flowers appear at the same time as gingery magnolia petals and perfumed osmanthus. Blended together, the trio make a unique floral tea. If you can't find osmanthus, you can buy dried flowers online. This recipe is for a dried tea, but it's also well worth using fresh flowers and buds. If you want to use fresh, use the petals from 1 camellia flower, 1 magnolia bud, 2 magnolia petals and 2 teaspoons of fresh osmanthus (or a pinch of dried) per cup.

To dry the flowers, harvest them on a dry day and gently pull the petals away from the flowerheads. Dehydrate on a low setting, making sure to lay out the petals without overlapping.

———————

MAKES 40G (1½OZ), ENOUGH FOR 10 CUPS
15g (½oz) dried camellia flowers
15g (½oz) dried magnolia flowers
1 teaspoon crumbled dried magnolia buds
1 teaspoon dried osmanthus flowers

Mix all the ingredients together in a bowl to combine, then spoon into an airtight jar.

To serve, use 1 teaspoon of the tea per cup and brew with just-boiled water for 5 minutes, or with cold water overnight.

This tea blend also makes a lovely perfumed syrup or infusion for cocktails.

Making the drinks

Concocting wild drinks can be as joyfully imprecise as throwing handfuls of herbs and flowers into a jug of water; but for preserving, fermenting and even drying plants, there are a number of steps that will make your drink-making sessions successful. The following section covers some of the more common processes along with suggestions of plants that lend themselves to each beverage. Some of the plants mentioned aren't featured in this book, but they are no less delicious than those that are.

Getting started

Turning edible wild plants into drinks can be as simple as putting them in a glass of water. But if you'd like to turn your hand to fermenting, infusing or storing your ingredients for a less abundant day, there are a few pieces of kit you'll want to have to hand. Fortunately, the essential paraphernalia for making wild drinks can be a frugal affair – a jug with a good pour, a cheap funnel, a large saucepan, a sieve, a straining cloth and, of course, bottles and jars to ferment and store your makes in. Grab your kit, and start turning botanicals into beverages.

Bottles and jars

Start collecting a box of glassware – beer, cider and other fermented drinks need strong bottles to withstand the pressure that can build up, so keep hold of the strong ones, especially if they have flip-top lids. Small brown bottles with a dropper or pipette lids are available from herbal suppliers, and not only give an apothecary style to your home bar, but also shield bitters and tinctures from light, keeping them at their best.

If you're infusing ingredients like berries or fermenting drinks, you'll need a selection of large, wide-necked jars. If you're using them for fermenting, make sure you have strong glass to withstand the pressure (it's worth investing in a few fermenting jars). If you're lucky enough to have a local deli, they often have stocks of empty gallon jars their pickles come in. Buy new lids for bottles or jars that have had strong flavours in them, or your delicate liqueurs could taste of pickled onions.

Keeping your ingredients submerged as they infuse or ferment can be the difference between success and failure. You can buy specially made fermenting glass weights or, alternatively, use a smaller jar that fits into the neck of your jar. If you don't have access to any of these, fill a plastic bag with water and push it into the top of the liquid to hold down the plants. Speaking of plastic, a selection of large plastic soda bottles are invaluable for keeping active ferments like champagnes and sodas in. They are less likely to explode under pressure and are easier to monitor, becoming taut when pressure needs releasing.

A yard of your finest cloth

Cheese or muslin cloths are essential for making clear drinks. You can buy small squares of muslin (cheese) cloth or jelly bags specifically for straining fruit, but if you have a haberdasher's nearby, look there first as cloth sold by the metre (or yard, according to where you are) will be far cheaper than that sold in cookshops. Buy a few metres and boil-wash before cutting it into squares of different sizes. The corners of large squares can be tied together to make a bag and hung from a hook – perfect for straining bulky malts and fruits.

For winemakers and brewers

If you want to make wine, cider or mead, you'll need containers with airlock lids. Most home brewers invest in a couple of 5 litre (8¾ pint) glass demijohns (carboys), but you could use glass bottles or even plastic drinks bottles, as long as an airlock bung can fit tightly in the neck. (See page 236 for more details on the equipment used in winemaking.)

Labels and notebooks

If you already make wild potions, you'll probably have a few unlabelled bottles at the back of your cupboard that you were so sure you'd remember what's in them. But now, months on, you probably have no idea, and the bottle has turned into a slightly feared no-go zone. Avoid such trauma by labelling your bottles as soon as you fill them.

At the very least, just write what your bottle contains and when you made it. But if your label is large enough, write down all the ingredients you've used (with volumes you used if you have them). If you're using a flavoured spirit, write down not just the type of spirit but also the brand – one gin is very different from another.

If your labels are too small to do this, make yourself a dedicated wild drinks notebook so you can share your delicious recipes. Or if you're more of a secretive type, keep it hidden like the makers of herbal liqueurs do.

Keeping clean

More important than fancy kit is making sure whatever you are using is thoroughly clean. The only bacteria you want to grow in your drinks are the good ones that make your drinks safe and delicious.

Buy a good bottle brush as it's really important to scrub any residue away from the insides of your bottles. Once sparkling clean, wash your equipment in very hot soapy water (or on the hottest setting of your dishwater). You can also soak your kit in sterilizing solution (the type used for babies' bottles is ideal) for up to a day before you use it – handy if you get called away before you can fill your clean bottles.

Storing

If you can't process your plants as soon as you have harvested them, put them into plastic containers lined with kitchen paper in the fridge where they will keep for a few days, sometimes over a week. If you want to store them for longer, the freezer is the modern wild drink maker's best friend – again, store your ingredients in well-sealed plastic boxes and freeze until you want to use them. A word of warning though: use them straight from the freezer, putting the frozen flowers or herbs straight into your liquids. If you let them thaw first, they'll become sludgy in texture and flavour.

Freezing juices, juice shots and cordials in large ice cube trays creates portion-sized cubes that you can take out as you need them.

All dried up

Drying is a great way to store your botanicals, especially for teas, coffees and infusions. Be aware, however, that the flavour of dried ingredients will be different to fresh ones.

You can dry herbs by hanging stems in loose bundles, or laying out on a tray on a radiator or even in a low oven. While a dehydrator is not an essential piece of kit, it's worth having to control the drying of plants – especially tender flowers and herbs that could burn, and plants with a high water content that could become mouldy. While you can invest in premium brands, cheap dehydrators work very well. (I have a ten-year-old dehydrator bought cheaply and have used it nearly every day through the summer and it is still going strong.) However you dry them, make sure they are completely dry before being stored – roots, twigs and barks should be brittle, flowers and herbs crumbly. If they don't crumble or break when crushed, you need to dehydrate them further. Keep your dried ingredients in airtight containers away from direct sunlight, replacing each year with the new harvest.

Safe storing

A lot of the processes in this book were originally created as a way to preserve seasonal harvests that are at their peak. The alcohol content in liqueurs, spirits and bitters prevents harmful bacteria from spoiling drinks, and fermentation will preserve drinks due to the creation of acids.

To make sure your ferments are acidic enough to be safe, they should have a pH value below 4.6. A pH monitor or pack of indicator strips is crucial if you want to make ferments.

If you want to store syrups and cordials by canning or pasteurizing them, there are a few things you can do to make sure they preserve well – use more sugar, make sure the pH level is below 4.6 and fill your bottles with the liquid while it is hot. There are a number of excellent guides to safe canning and pasteurizing available online or in print.

Pasteurizing jars and bottles

Place glass jars and bottles into a wide pan onto a trivet (or folded-up tea towel) placed on the bottom. Make sure they aren't touching each other, or the sides of the pan. Using water that is the same temperature as the jars, fill the pan so that the water comes two-thirds of the way up the sides of the jars. Heat until the water comes to a boil, then reduce the heat and simmer for 30 minutes. Using tongs, remove the jars from the pan and place upside down on a heatproof surface. Allow to cool and store in a cool place away from direct sunlight.

Country wines

Less well known than grape wine, but no less delicious and with an equally long history, are wines made from other fruits, flowers, herbs, tree leaves and even vegetables. Known today as 'country wines', these wines have a history of being drunk as medicinal aides, made to pull out the beneficial compounds in botanicals. Grapes became the go-to fruit to ferment because they contain the perfect blend of components needed for a successful and simple fermentation.

Fruits and botanicals are less easy to make into wine than grapes, rarely having enough sugar, the right balance of acid, or strain of yeast to simply 'press and go'. As the home winemaking masters will tell you, making wine with anything other than grapes will need the essential components of acid, sugar, tannin and yeasts, all tweaked to the right levels. It needs a more scientific approach than simply squashing grapes, but you'll be rewarded with a wine cellar full of diverse, delicious flavours.

Winemaking equipment

You don't need an army of bare-footed grape treaders or an air-conditioned cellar to become a home vintner, but you will need some essential equipment. Winemaking kits can be found cheaply in hardware stores and speciality brewing suppliers, and often for sale from retired homebrew enthusiasts. To make wine successfully, you will need the following:

- Food-grade container with a lid
- Sieve and muslin cloths
- Demijohns with airlocks and bungs (at least two)
- Tubes for siphoning
- Funnel
- Bottles and lids (if using corks, always use new ones)
- Bottle brush
- Hydrometer (see left)
- Testing jar
- Acid-testing kit (see left)

Hydrometers measure the density (known as specific gravity or SG) of liquids and show sugar and alcohol levels. Use at the start of the process and before bottling to help inform you of when fermentation has finished. A wine that has finished fermenting usually has a specific gravity reading between 0.96 and 0.99.

Acid-testing kits are used at the start and end of the winemaking process to make sure that the wine has enough acid to allow fermentation, and at the end to ensure it is not too acidic.

Additional ingredients

To maximize your chances of successful fermentation, creating a good flavour and avoiding unwanted bacteria, there are few extra ingredients that are advisable to add.

Sugar: Unlike grapes, most other fruits lack enough sugar on their own to make them ferment well. White cane sugar is widely added to country wines as it does not distract from the flavour of the main ingredient. Unrefined sugars ferment well but add a treacly flavour and work best in rich, fruity wines like blackberry and elderberry.

Acid: Yeast needs acid to ferment – often lacking in foraged fruits and herbs (and totally lacking in flowers). You can add acid by using lemon juice or a ready-made blend, usually made from malic, tartaric and citric acids. Test using an acid-testing kit at the start and end of the process – ideally, the reading should be between 0.55 and 0.65. If it is too high, you can reduce it by adding calcium or potassium bicarbonate, both of which are available from homebrew suppliers.

Tannin powder: Tannins add dryness and texture to wine. Tannin powder is made from grape skins. Add it before fermentation starts if you are using low-tannin ingredients. You can also use tea to add tannin, adding a strong cup of tea to every 4.5 litres (1 gallon) of liquid.

Campden tablets: These are made from potassium metabisulfite, otherwise known as sulfites. Potassium metabisulfite both kills any unwanted bacteria and stops wine from being spoiled by oxygen introduced during racking and bottling. A tablet is added 24 hours before the yeast, after racking and before bottling. You can also use them to sterilize equipment. If you are allergic to sulfites, don't use them but be extra careful about making sure your equipment and ingredients are very clean (and use an alternative sterilizing product).

Pectinase: This is an enzyme that breaks down pectin and helps to extract the maximum amount of juice from the fruit (especially useful for strawberries and plums). Adding it prior to fermenting also reduces haziness, and you can also add it later in the process.

Winemaking yeast: Fruits and botanicals don't always have the right yeast content to produce delicious flavours but you can add wine yeasts from a sachet. There are several available, but Champagne yeast is regarded as the best. Activate it 24 hours before using by mixing it in a bottle with a few tablespoons of grape or orange juice and a couple of teaspoons of sugar.

Yeast nutrients: The yeast in your wine will feed on sugars, converting them to alcohol. But yeasts also need other nutrients, which may be missing, especially in flower or herb wines. You can buy super yeasts, which contain yeast nutrients and kick-start fermentation quickly.

The winemaking process

1 Preparing your ingredients

Before your fruits, herbs or flowers can be turned into wine, they need to be sorted and cleaned to make sure that you are not using anything damaged or rotting, which could introduce unwanted bacteria.

2 Making the 'must'

Place the botanicals in a glass bottle or jar and add boiled water with sugar and additional acid (if necessary) to make a 'must'. This is the stage in winemaking where nothing has started fermenting yet. You are simply allowing flavours from the fruit, herbs or flowers to be pulled into the liquid.

3 The first fermentation

Add winemaking yeast to the bottle to start the fermentation and cover it with a muslin cloth and rubber band. Fermentation can take anything from a few days to over a week to start, depending on the type of wine.

4 Secondary fermentation

When the yeast starts converting sugars into alcohol, the wine will start forming bubbles on the surface. At this stage, strain it, removing any solids. Pour the liquid into a demijohn and seal with a clean airlock. You should see bubbles rise through the wine into the airlock after a couple of days.

5 Racking the wine

After a few weeks, the bubbles will stop rising. Separate (or rack) the wine from the sediment into a clean demijohn by siphoning it with a sterilized rubber tube. Add a crushed Campden tablet to your racked wine. You may need to rack the wine a second time if more sediment builds up. After racking, leave the wine to mature slowly: light, floral wines will be ready after a few months, dark fruit wines may need over a year.

6 Bottling the wine

Bottle the wine once it has matured. Fill bottles by siphoning the wine into them, leaving a small gap at the neck for the cork, if necessary. If using bottles with corks, store the bottles on their sides so that the corks stay wet and don't shrink.

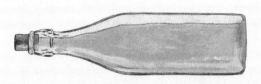

Beer

Beer today is usually made by fermenting the sugars in malted (or sprouted) grains, and flavoured with the bitter flowers of hop plants. But beer doesn't have to be made like this. In fact, hops were only introduced to beermaking a thousand or so years ago – that's fifteen thousand years after it's thought we first started brewing. Before hops dominated the scene, a wide range of different herbs were added to the drink, chosen according to their ability to preserve, flavour and even add psychotropic qualities. These kinds of beers are now known as gruit beers, or herbal beers.

Many wild plants can be used in brewing, including yarrow, mugwort, ground ivy, burdock, pine, spruce, camellia, Douglas fir and nettle. Those who avoid gluten can use gluten-free grains or even nuts like chestnuts and acorns instead of malted barley. You can also add wild fruits like hawthorn, rowan berries, plums and strawberries to beers to add subtle fruit flavours.

Ingredients and equipment

To make 10 litres (17½ pints) of your own malt and hop beer at home, you'll need the following ingredients and equipment:

- 1.25kg (2lb 12oz) malted (germinated) barley
- 30g (1oz) dried or 120g (4¼oz) freshly picked hops
- Large food-grade container (fermentation bucket or demijohn)
- Large saucepan
- Food thermometer
- Brewer's yeast
- Hydrometer to measure the alcohol
- Plastic tube for siphoning
- Beer barrel or beer bottles (flip-top lids are ideal)

Beer or soda?
The definition of a true beer is a drink brewed using malt. Some herbal beer recipes use white sugar instead of malt. This is often to make a beer with fresh, light flavours like the nettle beer on page 35. These kinds of beers sit halfway between a soda and a beer – you can choose how you label your bottle.

How to make beer with whole malt and hops

1 Making a mash
Place malted barley grains and water in a large saucepan and keep at 75°C (167°F) for an hour to release the sugars into the water, making what is called a mash.

2 Sparging
Transfer to another container, then strain the liquid through a bag or cloth back into the pan. Pour more warm water over the grains into the pan to extract any remaining sugar (this is called sparging).

3 Adding hops
Add dried or freshly picked hops to the pan, then bring the liquid up to the boil. Boil for 1 hour, then allow to cool to 21°C (70°F).

4 Fermentation
Once cool, strain the liquid through a fine sieve into a fermentation bucket or demijohn with an airlock. Swirl the liquid to increase its oxygen content, then add a packet of brewer's yeast. Leave the beer in a warm place to ferment for 4–14 days, until the bubbling stops. You can use a hydrometer to measure the alcohol content.

5 Bottling the beer
Transfer the beer to sterilized bottles, adding a teaspoon of sugar to each bottle before sealing. The beer is usually ready to drink after a week.

Non-alcoholic fermented drinks

A few years ago, the words 'kombucha' and 'kefir' would have made most people scratch their heads. But over the last decade, a fermentation revolution has been happening all across the world and now it's completely normal to drink sour teas and even fizzy milks. You'd be forgiven for thinking that these fermented drinks were a new invention but in fact for millennia, many different cultures of people across the world have used different cultures of beneficial bacteria to ferment health-giving drinks.

Fermented beverages aren't usually drunk to intoxicate, but instead to support our health. Made with probiotic microbes, which both feed our gut bacteria and nourish our bodies, fermented drinks have suddenly become almost obligatory for anyone interested in their wellbeing. Originally, many of these drinks were made to preserve ingredients, including milk. The yogurt in your fridge? That was first made as a drink to keep milk safe for longer.

Wild soda

Many wild ingredients have so many yeasts occurring naturally on them that you can simply plunge your botanicals into a jar, cover with water and a small amount of sugar, and within days you'll have a fizzy drink – a wild soda (like the Spruce needle soda on page 217).

If they are consumed after a few days, these drinks will have a tiny amount of alcohol in them, but no more than a glass of orange juice. Leave them to ferment for longer, though, and they'll create more alcohol – turning from a soda (which is traditionally, rather controversially, called a 'champagne') into a drink as alcoholic as cider. If you leave your soda to keep fermenting, it will turn into a wine.

Wild sodas are a great way of making drinks that taste of your local area, your own *terroir*. If you want to make drinks using your local plants, but inspired by elsewhere, listed opposite are some of the best-loved ferments from around the world to which you can add your own wild harvest.

Low alcohol, non-alcoholic and alcohol-free drinks

While these fermented drinks aren't considered alcoholic, there are small amounts of alcohol in them – drinks containing less than 0.5% alcohol are regarded as non-alcoholic and can be labelled as such. Since alcohol is created when fruits ripen, even orange and apple juices contain around 0.5% alcohol (the same as fermented drinks). They are regarded as safe, even for children, and you'd struggle to get drunk on either. If you want to avoid alcohol altogether, only drinks labelled 'alcohol free' are truly free from it.

Ferments from around the world

Kombucha: Hailing from China, this is made by fermenting black tea using a SCOBY (a symbiotic culture of bacterial yeasts). Buy or beg a SCOBY to use, but once you have one, you can use it for years. It is often made with two fermentations: first adding your SCOBY to sweet tea; second adding flavours. There are many wild plants to try, including camellia flowers, magnolia, honeysuckle, rose petals, blackberries, elderberries and pine needles.

Milk kefir: Drunk across the Caucasus for thousands of years, milk kefir is made by adding grain-sized clumps of bacteria to milk. These clumps are called kefir grains and are thought to have originally developed inside the leather bags that milk was carried in. You'll need to buy your first kefir grains but they'll grow fast. Milk kefir is delicious flavoured with fruit purées or flower syrups – try adding blackberries, wild strawberries, wild plums, clover flowers, rose petals or elderflower syrup.

Water kefir (or tibicos): It's thought that water kefir first came from fermenting cactuses in Mexico (where the drink is known as tibicos) which were added to sweetened water to ferment. Flavours are added during a second fermentation – try adding crab apples, sloes or herbs like linden flowers, elm seeds, fennel, mint, nettle, primrose or rose petals.

Kvass: Coming from Eastern Europe, kvass was originally made with rye or barley. It's now made with toasted bread, fruit, honey, beetroot and even birch sap. Try making kvass using wild cherries, or blending rosehips with beetroot.

Ginger beer: From the Caribbean, ginger beer is made using yeasts from the skin of ginger, which are turned into a starter called a bug. This is fed and added to liquids to create healthy fizzy drinks (not just ginger beer). While you have to source a SCOBY or kefir grains, you can make your own ginger bug at home (see page 244).

Tepache: A delicious Mexican fermented drink made with pineapple skins and leaves, which are covered in wild yeasts. Often flavoured with star anise and cinnamon, tepache can also be made with wild flavours like elderflower, linden, mint, wild oregano (*Origanum vulgare*), lemon balm (*Melissa officianalis*), bee balm (*Monarda*) and of course pineapple weed.

Sima: This quick-fermented lemonade hails from Finland. Made with Champagne yeast, it's ready to drink within a few hours. Try flavouring the drink with a few hop flowers, juniper or birch leaves.

Amazake: This is a sweet Japanese drink made by fermenting brown rice. Warming and creamy, it's often flavoured with anything from chocolate to fruit syrups. Try flavouring amazake with puréed rosehips or hawthorns.

Hardaliye: This fermented grape drink from Turkey is made with grapes, mustard seeds and cherry leaves soaked in grape juice. Benzoic acid (from tree resin) stops the drink from becoming alcoholic.

How to make a ginger bug starter

Ginger bugs are the base for ginger beer, but can also be added to a wide range of other drinks. One of the simplest ways to use a ginger bug is to add 100ml (3½fl oz) to a bottle of apple juice and within a few days you'll have a probiotic fizzy juice drink.

1 Preparing the ingredients
Coarsely grate a 5cm (2in) piece of unpeeled ginger into a glass jar and add 500ml (18fl oz) of unchlorinated water and 20g (¾oz) of unrefined sugar. Use organic ginger if possible for a more successful fermentation as regular ginger is often irradiated, which kills any beneficial bacteria.

2 Feeding the starter
Stir, cover with a cloth secured with a rubber band or string and place somewhere warm. Feed your starter daily by stirring in another 5cm (2in) piece of ginger, grated, 20g (¾oz) of sugar and 50ml (2fl oz) of water, and cover again with your cloth.

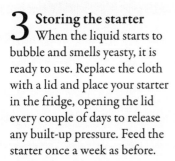

3 Storing the starter
When the liquid starts to bubble and smells yeasty, it is ready to use. Replace the cloth with a lid and place your starter in the fridge, opening the lid every couple of days to release any built-up pressure. Feed the starter once a week as before.

4 Apple and ginger soda
Use the starter bug to make an apple and ginger soda by straining 50ml (2fl oz) of it into 1 litre (1¾ pints) of apple juice in a strong bottle. Allow to ferment for 2–5 days until it is effervescent.

5 Making a simple soda
Try adding your starter to sweetened water along with herbs, flowers, fruits or other botanicals. You can also turn your cordials and herbal syrups into delicious fermented drinks by adding your ginger bug starter. Try flavouring your ferment with rosebay willow herb, birch leaves, camellia flowers or meadowsweet.

Cordials and syrups

Cordials and syrups are the all-rounders of the drinks cupboard, flavouring everything from water, coffees and teas to liqueurs, ferments and, of course, cocktails. The first syrups were made with honey, which was poured over herbs and flowers to preserve them for that all-too-common drink origin story – medicinal uses. Today they're mostly made with white sugar, which, while one of the least beneficial of sweeteners for health, is a great base for showcasing other flavours. Flavoured syrups can be far more than just sweetness; infused with everything from bitter roots to delicate flowers, they transform any drink into which they are drizzled.

Syrup or cordial?

Cordials are a type of syrup (apart from those of you who are reading in North America, for whom 'cordial' is a usually a sweet alcoholic liqueur; we'll come to those later). Whereas syrups can be simply made from sugar and water, cordials are always flavoured and include acidity (and sometimes salt). Elderflower syrup, for example, is simply made by infusing flowers into a sugar syrup whereas elderflower cordial has the addition of lemon juice or citric acid.

Both syrups and cordials can be flavoured with fruits, flowers, herbs, nuts, spices and even bitter botanicals (to make tonic syrups). They'll store in the fridge for a few weeks, or can be frozen in ice cube trays and pots to use later in the year. If you want to store your syrups for a longer time, you can pasteurize them – but they'll need to have a pH lower than 4.6 to store safely.

With most fruit syrups, the fruit is cooked first in order to release its liquid. However, you can make an uncooked syrup by macerating your ingredients in sugar (see the cheong recipe on page 97).

> If you prefer not to use refined sugar, try making syrups with light honey or unrefined (golden) sugar. You can also use sweeteners such as xylitol, but these will only keep for a few days.

How to make a fruit syrup

Fruit cordials and syrups are best made by cooking the fruit before adding sugar but herbal and floral ones are made by infusing the ingredients into pre-made syrup bases (see page 248).

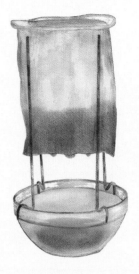

1 Preparing the fruit
Thoroughly wash the fruit, discarding any that is damaged or overripe.

2 Cooking the fruit
Place the fruit in a saucepan, adding a splash of water to soft fruits such as blackberries and elderberries. Completely cover harder fruits like apples, rosehips and hawthorns with water. Cook the fruit until it has broken up completely, adding more water if necessary.

3 Mashing and draining
Squash the fruit with a masher, then leave to soak in the liquid for an hour or so. Pour the mixture into a jelly bag (or a sieve lined with a muslin cloth), letting the juice drip into a bowl.

4 Making the syrup
If you want to add herbs or flowers to the syrup, add them now and allow the liquid to cool, then strain again. Measure the juice and pour into a clean saucepan, adding the same weight of sugar as fruit juice – for example, add 100g (3½oz) of sugar to every 100ml (3½fl oz) of juice. Bring to a boil and simmer, stirring, until all the sugar has dissolved, then transfer to a sterilized bottle.

How to make a flower syrup

The flavours of delicate flowers or herbs can be damaged by heat, so add your botanicals to just-hot syrups, leaving them to infuse as the liquid cools down to capture their flavour at its peak

1 Harvest your flowers
Some flowers hold flavour in their petals (roses, for example) and can be rinsed without losing any of it. Others, like elderflower, hold flavour in their pollen and nectar so it is best not to wash them. Remove the flowers from the stems before laying them in a shallow tray in the shade for about 30 minutes to allow any insects to crawl away to the light.

2 Make the syrup
Heat equal amounts of sugar and water (or twice the amount of sugar to water if you want to make a heavy syrup) in a pan until the sugar dissolves completely. Turn down the heat to a low setting and add strained citrus juice (if using). Remove the pan from the heat.

3 Add the flowers
When the syrup has cooled enough to touch, stir in the flowers, cover with a lid and leave to infuse for a few hours before straining.

4 Fill the bottles
Gently reheat the strained, infused syrup and pour into sterilized bottles.

Flavoured spirits, liqueurs and wines

For as long as we've been distilling spirits and fermenting wines, we've been adding flavourings to them. If it's edible, it's probably been infused into liquor (spirit) or wine at some point, turning the base liquid into one of a vast array of unique drinks that range from sweet, floral and fruity, to herbal, bitter and nutty. In fact, without wild plants, we wouldn't have many of the drinks we sip today – juniper-flavoured gin and wormwood-bittered vermouth wouldn't exist, and neither would Martini cocktails – a thought not worth thinking.

Just as bitters started life as medicinal potions, so flavoured liqueurs and wines have healers of old to thank, as they were made originally to preserve medicinal herbs in liquid. Unlike bitters, which are too strong to drink by themselves, liqueurs and wines were usually created with sugar to make them go down well.

Spirit or liquor, liqueur or cordial?

Making infused spirits and wines is a reassuringly easy thing to do, but more complicated are all the names the drinks have, especially if you're following recipes from different countries. So, before you infuse your tipple, here is a run-down of the liquids that make the drinks.

Base spirits: Also known as liquors, these are made by separating out the alcohol from fermented drinks like wine and cider. This is done in a still where the liquid is heated until the alcohol evaporates and is captured. At this stage, the alcohol (or distillate) is so strong it needs to be diluted to be safe to drink. We usually buy spirits diluted to less than 50 per cent alcohol by volume (ABV). The resulting drinks are 'base spirits' or 'base liquors' and include vodka, brandy, grappa, rum, eau de vie and whisky.

Flavoured spirits: These are made by adding flavouring ingredients to base spirits or liquors and include drinks like gin and aquavit.

Flavoured liqueurs: These are sweeter and less alcoholic than flavoured spirits as the base spirit is diluted with sugar and water. Flavoured liqueurs can be made with herbs, nuts, flowers or fruit. In America, liqueurs are often called cordials (cordials in other parts of the world are alcohol-free syrups) and some liqueurs are called crème liqueurs (such as crème de violette and crème de mûre). In this context, 'crème' doesn't refer to cream but to the creamy mouthfeel of the drink due to its high sugar content.

Just as vermouths can be made with either red or white wine, experiment using different types of wines in your infusions – the same botanical will taste very different in red, white, dry and sweet wines. For example, woody, warming herbs pair well with reds, whereas slightly bitter, aromatic herbs are lovely in sweet wines.

A lot of flavoured liqueurs use neutral spirits like vodka as the base liquid, but don't be afraid of using more strongly flavoured spirits like rum, brandy or whisky. Their distinctive taste often brings out the flavours of wild ingredients – gorse flowers, for example, are delicious infused into rum.

Flavoured or aromatized wines: These are made by infusing botanicals into wine and include drinks like Campari and vermouth. Flavoured wines vary in their alcohol content – less strong drinks are simply made by infusing botanicals into less strong wines.

Fortified wines: These have a higher alcohol content as spirits are added to help preserve the drink for longer. Some fortified wines also have sweetness added to them. If you want to sweeten your wine, you'll definitely need to add a spirit too as the sugar could start the wine fermenting again.

Attention to detail

Although making infused spirits and wines essentially just involves soaking your chosen ingredient in a spirit or wine, adding sweetness according to taste, there are things that can go wrong. For example, letting your ingredients oxidize or soak for too long can ruin what would be a beautiful tipple. To avoid this disastrous outcome, make sure your ingredients are submerged fully while soaking. Use a fermentation weight to press them down if needed, and keep tasting – as soon as it tastes of your chosen ingredient, strain off the liquid. Delicate herbs and flowers can take as little as an hour or two to infuse, soft fruits a week or so, hard berries and nuts up to a few months.

You can add sugar at the start of the infusion, but adding sugar at the end offers greater control over the sweetness, allowing you to get your sweetness just right.

Centerbe – one hundred herb liqueur – is an Italian drink made to a secret recipe with over a hundred different herbs. While you might not have that many in your basket, in the spring and summer herbs and edible flowers are in abundance and they can all be blended with a spoonful of honey, a pinch of cinnamon and nutmeg, and infused into wild herbal liqueurs.

How to make a sweet liqueur

1 Preparing the ingredients
Large hard fruits like crab apples can benefit from being cut in half or freezing to break open the skins and soften their flesh. Remove any bitter parts of flowers (rose petals, for example, have bitter tips).

2 Filling the jars
Put the fruit, plants or flowers into jars and cover with your chosen alcohol. If they rise to the surface, add a weight to keep them submerged. Place away from direct sunlight (unless making an instant liqueur like Instant elderflower limoncello, see page 69). Should you want to add sugar early on, add it now.

3 Infusing to taste
Taste regularly – herbs and flowers will infuse very quickly, especially in high-alcohol spirits. Rose petals can infuse within hours, creating a delicious floral spirit, but if left too long their bitter, tannic compounds will be extracted as well and your liquid will taste like cardboard rather than beautiful blooms. Once infused, strain the liqueur through a fine sieve into a bottle. If you haven't added sugar yet, you can use a coffee filter to strain out any fine particles.

4 Adding sweetness
Add sugar to the liqueur, stir and taste. If necessary, add more until you have your desired sweetness.

Tea

*The majority of cups of tea are made
with the leaves from one plant:* Camellia
sinensis. *This one plant is made into
green tea, matcha, oolong, white tea
and of course the famous black tea.
So ubiquitous is the camellia drink that
the term 'tea' is often held sacrosanct
for this one plant; but wild tea drinkers
know that it is just one of a bounty of
wonderful botanicals that the drink
can be made from.*

Wild tea can be made with everything from roots, seeds, barks and twigs through to fruit, flowers and leaves. It can be made as a warming hot drink or a cooling cold beverage, drunk simply for the pleasure of being a delicious form of hydration, or for specific health and wellbeing support.

Teas are regarded by herbalists as among the most effective ways of accessing the many benefits of botanicals. From the lupine in hops for better sleep, menthol in mint to soothe stomachs, the essential oil in fennel seed that supports digestion, to the immune-boosting properties of chaga fungi, a cup of herbal tea will provide far more than a comforting brew.

Fresh or dried?

Wild ingredients are often at their peak when they are most needed – elderflower, rose and yarrow with their cooling properties are in season in the heat of midsummer, while red deadnettle (*Lamium purpureum*) with its warming, circulation-boosting compounds flowers through the winter and early spring months. Using freshly gathered ingredients not only creates vibrant-tasting teas but also offers the added benefit of health-supporting bio-active compounds which include polyphenols and phytochemicals.

Sometimes though, you may want to reach for the benefits of a summer-gathered herb in the depths of winter, when the plant has receded underground. This is the time to reach for your dried teas. Drying preserves them for use later in the year when they might be needed but not available to gather.

Herbal teas not only offer medicinal balms, but also complex flavours – bitter, floral, earthy, sweet and fruity. A splash of a strong tea can add a delicious botanical element to cocktails, especially those that are non-alcoholic, replacing the flavours of drinks like gin.

The tea-making process

Drying the botanicals

To dry your harvests, spread them out on a drying rack in a dehydrator or on a radiator. Alternatively, place them in a fabric drying net hung in a well-ventilated place such as an airing cupboard. Tender herbs and flowers need very gentle heat of around 45–50°C (113–122°F) to retain their properties, and may only need a few hours to dry. Denser, woody ingredients like roots, barks and even fruits require warmer temperatures of 60–70°C (140–158°F) and will take a longer time to dry, sometimes a few days.

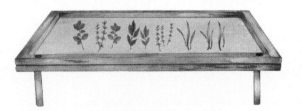

Storing the tea

Once you have dried your botanicals, place them in airtight jars and store them away from direct sunlight. You can keep them indefinitely but ideally replace them every year with the new season's harvest. When making teas with dried ingredients, use about one-third of the amount that you would when using fresh herbs – a teaspoon per cup is usually enough.

Making a hot infusion

The quickest and most common way to make tea is by pouring just-boiled water over botanicals and leaving them to infuse for 5–10 minutes before straining and drinking. This way of making tea is best for leaves, flowers and seeds, especially for those that are dried. Hot water, by its nature, semi-cooks the tea, changing flavours and releasing tannins from the ingredients. If left to infuse too long, it can turn an initially fresh, vibrant-tasting tea into a more robust, astringent drink.

Herbs and flowers like nettles, linden, thyme, mint, hawthorn leaves, hops, honeysuckle and, of course, camellia make delicious hot-infused teas.

Making a cold infusion

Cold brewing tea is a slower process. Soak fresh botanicals in cold water overnight before straining and drinking to allow more of the beneficial compounds of fresh herbs to dissolve into the water. Cold brewing releases fewer tannins, creating a less astringent, often sweeter tea. Nettle leaves, for example, release a lemony, sweetly floral flavour when infused overnight. These floral flavours make cold-brew teas especially useful ingredients in cocktails.

Botanicals that work well in cold brews include most flowers, herbs like cleavers and nettles, young tree leaves and blossoms. Certain tougher botanicals also benefit from cold infusion, including elm seeds. Cold infusions can be stored in the fridge for a couple of days after making them.

Making decoction teas

Some harder ingredients need to be simmered in hot water to release their taste and beneficial compounds. Make a decoction by chopping the ingredients and placing in a saucepan with a cup of water for every tablespoon of botanicals. Cover with a lid, bring to a boil and simmer for 20 minutes. Leave to sit for another 10 minutes before drinking. You can refrigerate decoctions for a couple of days and reheat before serving.

Botanicals that work well in decoctions include magnolia bark, birch twigs, chicory, dandelion and burdock roots, elderberry, wild cherry, fennel, burdock, hawthorn berries, rosehips, liquorice, rosemary, pine, fir and juniper. Chai is a form of decoction.

Juices and smoothies

From algae-infused juices to bright blue smoothies, these drinks are so much part of our diets that whole refrigerated aisles in shops are devoted to the vibrantly coloured bottles. One of the reasons that the drinks are so popular is that they are an incredibly quick way to get nutrition into our bodies, especially those of busy people and fussy eaters. A plethora of incredible-sounding botanicals from a shop in a plastic bottle might be easy and quick, but making them yourself is almost as easy. You also have the benefit of knowing exactly what is in your drink, and can use up a glut from your garden or even the fruit bowl, which might otherwise be at risk of being wasted.

You don't have to own a juicer – a blender will make a pulpy drink complete with health-giving fibres. Leave them in for a smoothie, or strain the mixture through a sieve to make a juice. You can even use a box grater or pestle and mortar to break down ingredients.

There is another way to extract juices and this is by using heat to break open the fruits – effectively stewing it. You also get the bonus of cooked fruit that can be used in a whole host of dishes.

Juice ingredients
How you make your juice will be guided not only by the equipment you have, but also by the kind of ingredients you are using.

Soft fruits: These include blackberries, raspberries, mulberries and wild blueberries and they are so full of liquid that after a day in a tub, they'll start to sit in their own bright juice. Process them by pressing, heating or puréeing. Strawberries and wild strawberries have spongy flesh that holds onto its juices. Macerate them by chopping them into small pieces and coating with a layer of sugar; cover and leave overnight.

Hard fruits: These include crab apples, wild pears and quinces. They are too hard to press whole, so chop or grate the fruit into very small pieces before blending and extracting the juice. Be aware that the juice and flesh of these fruits will oxidize and turn brown quickly, so add a squeeze of lemon juice or a pinch of citric acid to help keep their colour.

'Dry' fruit: These include hawthorns, sloes and rosehips, which are rich in flavour but have very dry flesh. These fruits are best processed by heat or by blending with the addition of another liquid (apple juice is ideal) and using a blade that won't break open the seeds. If making a juice with rosehips, make sure to use a very fine cloth to strain the juice as the fine hairs in the fruits are irritants.

Leaves and flowers: These include sorrel, nettle, pine needles, hawthorn leaves, rose petals, linden flowers and leaves, honeysuckle and clover flowers and leaves.

Often rich in vitamins and minerals, along with compounds like antioxidants, anti-inflammatories and other beneficial properties, herbs, leafy greens and flowers might not offer much liquid but are great ingredients in juices and smoothies. If you are using stems or leaves in a blender, roughly chop the plants before adding them to avoid the stems from wrapping around the blades. As well as being used fresh, they can be dried and ground into powders to add to smoothies later in the year when fresh harvests aren't available.

Nuts: Adding nuts such as hazelnuts, walnuts, beech nuts and chestnuts to juices and smoothies adds flavour, texture and a vast array of nutritional benefits. Soaking nuts to make juices (or nut milks) and to blend into smoothies not only helps to make them easier to process and blend, but also increases the amount of nutrition that we are able to absorb from them.

Storing juices and smoothies

Juices and smoothies are best drunk fresh as they can start oxidizing and turning brown very quickly. Store them in the fridge where they will keep fresh for a couple of days, or in the freezer for up to three months. Fruit juices can also be preserved for longer by canning (or pasteurizing).

Although juices are often drunk chilled, they also make great warming drinks. In certain traditional medicines such as Ayurvedic and Traditional Chinese Medicine, during the winter people are advised to drink warming drinks rather than cold. Juices make lovely mulled drinks, often with the addition of warming spices such as ginger, star anise and clove.

How to make fruit juice using heat

Extracting juice from fruits by cooking them in water makes a drink that can be stored and has the added benefit of cooked fruit to eat. These drinks, called kompots, are drunk ice cold with herbs such as mint, fennel and lemon balm, or warm with spices.

1 Processing the fruit
Wash your fruit and chop up large pieces. Discard any that are bruised or damaged. Weigh it, then add the same volume of water as weight of fruit. For example, add 100ml (3½fl oz) of water to every 100g (3½oz) of fruit. Cover and heat until the fruit becomes very soft, cooking it on the lowest setting for 30 minutes (you can use a slow cooker for this).

2 Sweetening
Take the pan off the heat and taste your liquid – if it's too sour, sweeten with a sweetener of your choice such as a light honey, sugar or dried raisins. Stir the sweetener into the liquid and let it cool. Strain through a fine sieve or muslin cloth and pour the juice into a bottle. The fruit can be kept in a jar in the fridge for up to 3 days.

3 Preparing to preserve
If you'd rather preserve your juice and fruit for later in the year, half-fill sterilized jars with the fruit then pour over the juice until the jars are filled to just below the rim. Seal the jar with clean lids and pasteurize in a water bath (see page 235) or pressure canner.

Wild coffee

Every day, over two billion cups of coffee are drunk around the globe. Roasted and ground coffee beans are brewed into the dark, bitter drink that many of us have to consume before we can face the world. Although coffee itself is a rather beneficial herbal drink full of antioxidants and polyphenols, it also contains significant amounts of caffeine. While a small amount of caffeine is no bad thing, limiting how much we consume of it is a good idea. Fortunately, there are wild plants all around you that will take the beans' place and can be roasted into rich, bitter and delicious powders – just without the caffeine.

Don't expect your herbal coffee to be exactly like coffee. All herbal coffees have their own unique flavours, from woody to bitter, vanilla to earthy. Try mixing together plants to make a blend you like, and remember it's also fine to add coffee beans – good news if you can't face the day without caffeine. The following plant material can be successfully turned into coffee.

Roots

Dandelion, chicory and burdock roots are rich in inulin prebiotic fibre, which supports digestive (gut) health. Forage online for maca root powder (*Lepidium meyenii*), a member of the wild cabbage family that grows in the Andes. It is thought to boost energy, improve mood and boost metabolism.

Nuts

Acorn coffee is rich in nutrients and minerals and is thought to support blood and gut health. Beech nuts are rich in protein, vitamins, minerals and healthy fats. Hazelnuts and chestnuts are often blended with coffee, increasing the nutrition of the drink and adding a warming nutty flavour.

Seeds

Cleavers seeds contain a small amount of caffeine, support the lymphatic system and boost immunity (see the cleavers coffee recipe on page 221). Linden seeds have a smooth texture and delicious flavour, tasting somewhere between coffee and chocolate. Forage online for edible lupin seeds (*Lupinus albus* and *L. angustifolius*), baobab seeds (*Adansonia*) and date seeds (*Phoenix dactylifera*).

> Alongside wild plants, grains like wheat and barley, and mushrooms including chaga (*Inonotus obliquus*), reishi (*Ganoderma lingzhi*) and *Cordyceps militaris*, are often added to herbal coffee blends.

The coffee-making process

3 **Drying the plant matter**
Spread out the prepared ingredients on a tray lined with baking paper and place on a radiator or in a very low oven until dry. They have to be roasted to develop their flavour. This is done in an oven preheated to 150°C (300°F), Gas Mark 2. Roast until the pieces have turned brown, but not black.

1 **Preparing the ingredients**
Thoroughly wash roots, if you are using them, and discard any rotten nuts or seeds.

2 **Processing**
Chop any large roots or nuts into small pieces to allow them to dry evenly.

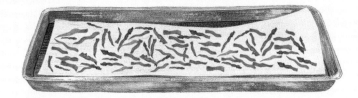

4 **Cooling and grinding**
Remove from the oven and cool. Place the dried and roasted ingredients into airtight jars until needed, then grind into a powder in small batches just before serving to ensure the coffee remains fresh.

5 **Making coffee**
Spoon a tablespoon of coffee powder per person into a cafetière; add a cup of just-boiled water per person, stir and let brew for 10 minutes before serving.

Vinegars

Like wine, beer and probiotic drinks, vinegar is made by the process of fermentation but the bacteria that make vinegar eat alcohol, creating (acetic) acid. If you've left an open bottle of wine, ferment or fruit juice for too long and it becomes sour, you've started to make vinegar. Although you wouldn't want to drink them neat, vinegars can be refreshing, hydrating and nourishing and have been consumed all over the world for many, many years. You can drink your vinegar by simply adding a splash into a cocktail, or flavouring it with honey or sugar, fruits or herbs before diluting in water.

Vinegars made from fruit or fruit juice tend to be slightly less acidic and more fruity than vinegars made from alcohol, so they are ideal to turn into drinks.

These are some of the most common flavoured drinking vinegars:

Shrubs: These are made by blending vinegar with sugar and fruits, either by heating them together or macerating for a few days before straining. Try making them with blackberries, wild plums, wild strawberries or rosehips.

Switchels: Hailing from the Caribbean, switchels are a blend of vinegar with ginger and a sweetener – sometimes honey, but often molasses or cane sugar. Try adding to fruit or flowers such as clover, elderflower, honeysuckle or meadowsweet.

Oxymels: Oxymels originated in ancient Greece and combine vinegar and honey with herbs, spices and fruits. Try making oxymels with sumac, wild thyme or nettles.

Sekanjabin: A Persian drink made by reducing vinegar, sugar and water into a concentrated syrup, and usually served diluted in ice-cold water with cucumber and mint. Try adding mint, rose petals, linden flowers or elm seeds.

How to make your own vinegar
You can make vinegar from alcohols such as wine, cider and even beer, by pouring the drink into a wide-necked jar, covering with a cloth and leaving somewhere warm to allow the bacteria to get busy. You can also make a new vinegar from the remains of a raw (or live) vinegar such as unpasteurized apple cider vinegar. This contains a colony of bacteria in a sediment or mother (that can form a thick disc on top of the liquid). Simply add this to a jar of fruit juice or chopped fruit.

How to make apple scrap vinegar

This kind of vinegar isn't acidic enough to pickle with, but is lovely used as a base for drinks like shrubs and switchels.

1 Preparing the apples
Three-quarters fill a sterilized jar with chopped apples and cover with unchlorinated water. Stir in a teaspoon of sugar; this will help start the fermentation of yeasts on the apple skins.

2 Starting fermentation
Cover the jar with a muslin cloth, and tie with a band. Place the jar in a warm room, stirring every day for a few days.

3 Straining the vinegar
Once it starts to bubble, strain the liquid into a second sterilized jar and cover again with the cloth. It will continue to bubble.

4 Bottling and sealing
Once the liquid stops bubbling, it should also have turned sour. Test its acidity with a pH indicator strip to make sure the pH level is below 4.6 – this is acidic enough to make sure the vinegar is safe and will preserve well. Pour it into a bottle and seal with a vinegar-proof lid.

Bitters

One sign you're in a good cocktail bar is the range of little bottles of bitters nestled among the spirits and mixers. Like many drinks, bitters date back thousands of years, when they were created as medicines. They only moved to bar shelves from the herbalists' apothecaries during the cocktail revolution, and have been associated with drinks ever since.

Bitters are too overpowering to consume neat, but a judicious single drop can almost miraculously make drinks taste brighter and more delicious. Both their intense flavour and herbal benefits come from botanicals with bitter compounds that have been steeped in a liquid (called a 'solvent') until it takes on their flavours. Bitters can be made with just a single ingredient, but are often made with a blend of (usually wild) herbs, spices, flowers, fruits and even nuts, barks and roots.

You can make bitters by simply soaking your ingredients all together in your chosen liquid. This is quick and uses just one jar. However, it also runs the risk of one flavour overpowering the rest and 'softer' ingredients being soaked for too long and their flavour being ruined.

The other way to make blends is to first infuse your ingredients individually before blending your bitters. The advantage of this is that you can add to your range of flavours over the year, creating a store of ingredients to access as you need them. If you're herbally inclined, you'll also be able to use the individual tinctures for their medicinal properties. Do you have itchy eyes from hay fever? Try drinking a glass of water with a few drops of elderflower tincture. Do you have a cut? Try dabbing it with yarrow tincture. You'll soon not only build up a wild drinks cupboard, but also a well-stocked apothecary.

Alongside true bitters that are added drop by drop into drinks, you'll also find some drinks referred to as 'bitters', such as vermouth, amaro, Aperol and nocino. Also known as digestifs, these are traditionally drunk after a meal to aid digestion. These drinks are often fortified wines, flavoured with bitter botanicals including artichoke, walnut and mugwort.

Alcohol-free bitters

While high-alcohol spirits are traditionally used to make bitters and tinctures, they are watered down to such an extent when used that many people are comfortable using them even in non-alcoholic drinks. But if you want to avoid alcohol completely, you can make bitters using glycerin, vinegar, sugar syrup or water. They'll have a slightly different flavour because the compounds that are soluble in alcohol aren't always soluble in other liquids. Be aware that bitters made just with water must be used within a couple of days as they won't keep.

Seasonal bitters

In spring: Try making fresh, grassy bitters with birch twigs, cherry bark, dandelion or burdock leaf paired with violets, sloe blossom and leaves, cleavers, hawthorn leaves, pine shoots, nettles, sorrel leaves, dock leaves and roots and rhubarb stems and roots.

In summer: Capture floral bitters with unripe walnuts, mugwort, yarrow and chamomile as your bitter flavours, paired with wild strawberries, cherries, fennel, wild thyme, meadowsweet, elderflower, honeysuckle, wild rose and apricot-flavoured agrimony (*Agrimonia eupatoria*).

In autumn: Mix bitter hops and acorns with berries such as hawthorn and sloes, along with spices like hogweed or cow parsnip (*Heracleum sphondylium*).

In winter: Blend woody, warming bitters using dandelion, burdock or mahonia roots with oak chips along with cleavers, rosehips, brown beech leaves, medicinal fungi like reishi and chaga, and warming clove-flavoured wood avens (*Geum urbanum*). Along with your gathered ingredients, bitters often contain more conventional herbs, spices and fruits including allspice, cardamom, clove, cinnamon, vanilla, pepper, lavender, rosemary, sage, citrus fruits (especially peels), dried fruits, cocoa and coffee beans.

How to make bitters

1 Planning a recipe
Work out the recipe for your bitters. Think about the kind of drinks you want to make – floral and herbal bitters work with gins, spiced and woody bitters with dark rum and whisky, for example. Blends of bitters usually have a combination of bitter, herbal, floral, spiced and fruity flavours.

2 Filling the jars
Place your ingredients into small jars. If you are using dried ingredients, use 1–2 teaspoons for each 100ml (3½fl oz) of spirit. If using fresh ingredients, use half the amount of botanical to volume of spirit. Cover with your chosen spirit – you can use any high-alcohol spirit but vodka is the least flavoured. Seal the bottles, label and date each jar and place away from direct sunlight to infuse.

3 Straining the tinctures
If you're using fresh flowers and herbs, taste them after a couple of hours of soaking. Once the alcohol becomes flavoured, strain through a fine filter into a small, labelled bottle or jar. Tougher ingredients will need longer to infuse – shake the bottles daily and taste every day to check for flavour. The bitter herb tinctures should become very strongly flavoured. Strain and bottle as the tinctures are ready.

4 Blending the bitters
Once all your tinctures have been made, you can start to make your blend. Up to half the blend will usually be made up of bitter tinctures; the rest from more floral, fruity, wood and herbal flavours. Start by placing 1 teaspoon of each of your tinctures in a jar, then mix and add more bitter tinctures or other flavours, according to taste. It's worth adding a drop of the bitters into a glass of water or apple juice to taste. If you need a stronger flavour, add more of the bitter tinctures.

5 Fine-tuning the blend
Some people also add bitter-flavoured waters to their bitters blend. These are made by heating water and botanicals in a pan for 10 minutes before leaving to infuse for a few hours. Use one part infused water to four parts alcohol-based tinctures, or more if your alcohol was very high proof (such as Everclear). You can also sweeten the bitters with honey or sugar by adding a teaspoon of sugar and dissolving it into the blend by shaking.

6 Storing bitters
Pour the mixture into an amber dropper bottle, label with the botanicals used and store out of direct sunlight.

Resources

Wild plant identification guides

Some of these cover globally available plants, others are written for specific areas.

Collins Wild Flower Guide, 2nd Edition, David Streeter (Collins, 2016)

Collins Tree Guide, Owen Johnson (Collins, 2006)

Harrap's Wild Flowers: A Field Guide to the Wild Flowers of Britain & Ireland, Simon Harrap (Bloomsbury, 2018)

Field Guide to the Wild Flowers of the Western Mediterranean, Chris Thorogood (Kew Publishing, 2021)

Botany in a Day: A Herbal Field Guide to Plant Families of North America, Thomas J Elpel (Hops Press, 2000)

A word on plant identification apps

Apps can be a great tool in your plant identification kit but they are not a substitute for your own knowledge. Although becoming more reliable, they can still make mistakes so always do further research on your plants before you eat them.

Wild food guides

Don't be put off buying a book if it's officially written for a different area, many of the edible wild plants may still grow near you.

Forage: Wild Plants to Gather, Cook and Eat, Liz Knight (Laurence King, 2021)

Sam Thayer's Field Guide to Edible Wild Plants of Eastern and Central North America, Sam Thayer (Foragers Harvest Press, 2023)

Edible Plants: A Forager's Guide to the Plants and Seaweeds of Britain, Ireland and Temperate Europe, Geoff Dann (Anthropozoic Books, 2022)

Forage, Harvest, Feast: A Wild-Inspired Cuisine, Marie Viljoen (Chelsea Green, 2018)

The Forager Chef's Book of Flora, Alan Bergo (Chelsea Green, 2021)

The New Wildcrafted Cuisine, Pascal Baudar (Chelsea Green, 2016)

Wild Food: A Complete Guide For Foragers, Roger Phillips (Macmillan, 2014)

Food For Free: 50th Anniversary Edition, Richard Mabey (William Collins, 2022)

The Forager's Calender, John Wright (Profile Books, 2020)

Foraging & Feasting: A Field Guide and Wild Cookbook, Dina Falconi (Botanical Arts Press, 2013)

Backyard Foraging, Ellen Zachos (Storey Publishing, 2013)

Herbal medicine books

As you will have seen throughout this book, wild drinks and herbal medicine go hand in hand.

The Handmade Apothecary, Vicky Chown and Kim Walker (Kyle Books, 2017)

The Herbal Remedy Handbook, Vicky Chown and Kim Walker (Kyle Books, 2019)

Wild Remedies, Rosalee de la Forêt and Emily Han (Hay House, 2020)

Hedgerow Medicine, Julia Bruton-Seal and Matthew Seal (Merlin Unwin, 2008)

Rosemary Gladstar's Medicinal Herbs, Rosemary Gladstar (Storey, 2012)

Herbal Elixirs, Sue Mullett and Jade Harris (The Crowood Press, 2021)

Cocktails, mocktails and more

If you want to explore your new-found wild drinks larder, the following books are well worth having.

Wild Cocktails From the Midnight Apothecary, Lottie Muir (Cico, 2015)

Ancient Brews: Rediscovered and Re-created, Patrick E. McGovern (W. W. Norton & Company, 2017)

The Wildcrafted Cocktail, Ellen Zachos (Storey, 2017)

Wild Drinks: The New Old World of Small-batch Brews, Ferments and Infusions, Sharon Flynn (Hardie Grant, 2023)

Slow Drinks, Danny Childs (Hardie Grant, 2023)

Wild Drinks and Cocktails, Emily Han (Fair Winds Press, 2015)

Booze for Free, Andy Hamiliton (Eden Project Books, 2011)

The Wildcrafting Brewer, Pascal Baudar (Chelsea Green, 2018)

Wildcrafted Fermentation, Pascal Baudar (Chelsea Green, 2020)

Forager's Cocktails, Amy Zavatto (HarperCollins, 2015)

Booze: River Cottage Handbook No. 12, John Wright (Bloomsbury, 2013)

DIY Bitters: Reviving the Forgotten Flavor, Guido Masé and Jovial King (Fair Winds Press, 2023)

Fermentation: River Cottage Handbook No. 18, Rachel de Thample (Bloomsbury, 2020)

Ferment From Scratch, Mark Diacono (Quadrille, 2022)

Online inspiration

Fine-tune your social media feed with these inspiring Instagram accounts.

@ediblealchemy.co – online fermentation courses.
@markwildfood – UK-based foraging guide with expertise in wild drinks
@practicalselfreliance – guide to herbalism and foraging
@foragecolarado – Orion Aon, foraging teacher
@leviobrien_trees – Levi O'Brien, tree identification expert
@marie_viljoen – Marie Viljoen, author and foraging guide
@choudharyvan – Vanika Choudhary, chef and forager based in Mumbai, India
@indigenousfoodlab – Promoting indigenous American food
@feralforaging – Jesse Akozbek – introduction to wild food

Index

About the author

Liz Knight is a leading wild plant and foraging expert who lives in the Black Mountains in Wales, UK. She runs courses and workshops in foraging and cookery, and is the author of the bestselling book *Forage: Wild Plants to Gather, Cook and Eat* (Laurence King, 2021). When not writing or teaching, she can usually be found deep in a ditch or hedge, surrounded by nettles and brambles. www.foragefinefoods.com

About the illustrator

Veronica Ballart Lilja is a Swedish illustrator based in New York. Her clients are mainly in the fields of fashion, textile, editorials, magazines, advertising, packaging and stamps. Most of Veronica's work is in watercolour, mixing different techniques. Her book *If You're Bored with Watercolour, Read This Book* (Octopus, 2017) has been translated into several languages. www.veronicaballart.com

Acknowledgements

To my lovely, patient husband and children. Thank you for drinking my brews, indulging my herbal cures and for letting me hide away to write this book. I love you all and am very proud of who you all are.

I'm not sure I'd have written any books if it wasn't for Zara Larcombe, who commissioned my first, *Forage*, and then *Wild Drinks*. I love working with you and being in your fold. Thank you for finding me when you did.

A book is only as good as it is because of its editors and I lucked out with mine: Virginia Brehaut, you're patient, kind and the type of person I could happily go on a long walk with. Thank you for working on *Wild Drinks* with me, I've loved every moment. Thank you also to Joanna Smith, copy editor extraordinaire, you made my words more eloquent but kept them mine – my ego and I thank you!

Hopefully by now, you've flicked through the book and seen the beautiful illustrations by Veronica Ballart Lilja; if ever an illustrator should be sainted for their patience, it's you. I dread to think how many 'tweaks' were asked for and always done with an email version of a smile. Thank you for your stunning watercolours – it's been so lovely receiving them and getting to know you.

Along with Veronica's beautiful illustrations the reason this book looks beautiful is down to Sarah Pyke, who stoically laid out the pages for months on end. Thank you for your skill and endurance!

Thank you to everyone who has supped on one of my wild drinks served at courses and wild feasts over the years. I hope you enjoy the book as much as I've enjoyed your company.

First published in the United Kingdom in 2024
by Skittledog, an imprint of Thames & Hudson Ltd,
181A High Holborn, London WC1V 7QX

Concept and layout © Thames & Hudson 2024

Text © Liz Knight 2024
Illustrations © Veronica Ballart Lilja 2024

British Library Cataloguing-in-Publication Data
A catalogue record for this book is available from
the British Library

ISBN 978-1-837-76013-8

Printed and bound in China by C and C Offset
Printing Co., Ltd

Senior Editor: Virginia Brehaut
Designer: Sarah Pyke
Production: Felicity Awdry

Be the first to know about our new releases,
exclusive content and author events by visiting:

skittledog.com
thamesandhudson.com
thamesandhudsonusa.com
thamesandhudson.com.au